AF530026

UNDERSTANDING MUTUAL FUNDS

A Guide to Wealth Creation

UNDERSTANDING MUTUAL FUNDS

A Guide to Wealth Creation

DR. AASHKA THAKKAR

red'shine
Publication

UNDERSTANDING MUTUAL FUNDS: A GUIDE TO WEALTH CREATION
Author: DR. AASHKA THAKKAR

■

RED'SHINE PUBLICATION PVT. LTD.
Headquarters (India): 88, Patel Street, Navamuvada,
Lunawada, India-389 230
Contact: +91 76988 26988
Registration no. GJ31D0000034

In Association with,
RED'MAC INTERNATIONAL PRESS & MEDIA. INC
India | Sweden | Canada

■

Text © *Author*, 2021
Cover page ©RED'SHINE Studios, Inc, 2021

■

All right reserved. No part of this publication may be reproduced or used in any form or by any means- photographic, electronic or mechanical, including photocopying, recording, taping, or information storage and retrieval systems- without the prior written permission of the author.

■

ISBN: 978-93-90937-33-2
ISBN-A: 10.978.90937/332
DIP: 18.10.332/90937
DOI: 10.25215/9789390937332
Price: ₹ 200/-
April, 2021 (First Edition)

■

The views expressed by the authors in their articles, reviews etc. in this book are their own. The Editor, Publisher and owner are not responsible for them. All disputes concerning the publication shall be settled in the court at Lunawada.

■

www.redshine.co.in | info@redshine.in
Printed in India | Title ID: 90937332

With the blessings of
"LORD KRISHNA"

Preface

"A Successful Investment is Managing Risk and not Avoiding it" – Benjamin Graham

This introductory guide seeks to reflect the growth and importance across the globe of mutual funds as an avenue of investment.

The main objective is to provide the readers with a basic understanding of mutual funds, about its mechanism and the way it works. Also, the book provides an insight on the Indian Mutual Fund Industry, its Growth, and the basic terminology of Mutual Funds.

The book also guides the investors with the major reasons for selecting the mutual funds for their wealth creation, different funds available in the market, how to select the right fund and so on.

I am indebted to the industry's trade bodies, statistical firms and regulatory authorities for placing so much helpful material on their web-sites, sources that I heartily commend to any serious student or potential investor.

Neither the publishers nor I accept any responsibility for actions, claims or losses arising out of the use of information contained in this guide.

"Mutual Funds give people the sense that they are investing with the big boys and that they're really not at a disadvantage entering the Stock Market" – Ron Chernow

Acknowledgement

My Life is so blessed with some of the most amazing people. Thank you all for being part of my Journey.

Writing a book harder than I had thought and more rewarding I could have ever imagined. This would not have been possible with the endless support, love and blessings of my Family and Friends. Let me first thank to the Source of my Inspiration, My Darling Daughter- Devanshi. She has been my lucky charm and my source of positive energy.

My journey of becoming an Author is incomplete without the Support, Guidance and Criticism of my loving husband Hardik Thakkar. The constant push, motivation after every negative moment, and a healthy criticism has led to reach this outcome, of me becoming a proud Author.

Behind Every successful daughter there are Proud and Encouraging Parents. Its difficult to put in to words, how thankful I am to my parents Mrs. Anita Patel and Mr. Himanshu Patel for making me who I am today.

The List is incomplete without thanking enough my ever-supporting In-laws, Mr. Jagdishbhai Thakkar and Mrs. Vilashben Thakkar for always motivating and pouring their blessings on me to excel in Life.

Finally, thanking my sister, family members, friends and colleagues for being a part of my journey.

A Special thanks to my Publishing Team for their support.

Dr. Aashka Thakkar

Contents

Chapter 1

Introduction to Mutual Funds

The advertisement of Mutual Fund says that **"Mutual Investment are Subject to Market Risk"** But if one selects the right fund matching their financial goals, for the right tenure **"Mutual Funds Sahi He"**. Mutual Funds are the ideal source of investment specifically for the small investors, as they can get benefit of investing in a large number of stocks in the ocean of stock market with a minimum risk and a portfolio having a potential of getting higher returns than the traditional risk investment avenues.

Mutual Fund is an investment instrument which mobilizes the savings of small investors and this pool of money is invested in different securities, which in turn provides returns and capital appreciation to the investors. The gains or losses are shared by the investors as per their proportionate investment and holding in the scheme. The mutual funds are run by different Asset Management Companies (AMC's). Each AMC offers a variety of mutual fund schemes suited as per the need of investors.

Investment has been a crucial decision for individual investors since ancient times. Purchase of some asset from the surplus of income over expenditure to generate more money is investment. In other words, investment can be defined as the commitment of funds to one or more assets that will be held over some future time period. In Graham's words "Investment is putting money into something upon thorough analysis, with the expectation of gain that has a high degree of security for the principal amount, as well as security of return, within an expected period of time". Therefore, it entails arriving at numerous decisions such as investment amount, type of securities and timing. All investment choices are made in accordance with personal investment needs and in consternation of an uncertain future. Further such decision making has to be persistent and rational.

The Indian financial market has been successful enough from the past two decades from offering a variety of financial instruments in the market. The Indian mutual fund industry has grown rapidly since last 25 years. People have started realizing mutual fund as one of the key investment avenues to reach their financial goals. The best part is that, the growth of mutual funds is not only restricted to urban parts but has also managed to tap the semi urban and how the rural parts as well. Mutual funds have risen up as vital financial instrument which is benefitting both the investors and the capital markets.

The share of Indian mutual fund industry compared with the major industries like U.S.A, Europe and Asia Pacific is just like a drop of water in the ocean. However, the Indian mutual fund industry has shown a robust growth in term of its assets under management in the past decade. Over the past decade, the Indian mutual fund industry has grown almost at a double role that the major mutual fund industries in the world. The investors have now changed their focus from the traditional investment avenues to mutual funds i.e., AUM to bank deposits have raised from 13% in 2016 to 22% in 2018. Considering the current scenario regarding the investment in mutual funds, the total AUM data of open-ended schemes in 2018 reveals that the debt funds tops with an investment of 50%, followed by equities 30% and 14% investment in hybrid funds.

The AUM as on 30th June 2019 stands to Rs. 24.25 trillion as compared to 9.75 trillion in June 2014, which shows a 4 times growth of the industry in just 5 years. If we compare the growth of the Indian Mutual Fund industry in the growth rate of other region, we find that in the past decade when the Indian mutual fund industry witnessed a 12.5% CAGR, on the other Asia-pacific including India grew only 8% for the same time period.

The mutual fund industry has contributed largely to the growth of Indian capital markets, as the investment in mutual Funds has increased from 8.5% in 2014 to 18.4% in 2018. To an utter surprise, the rapid growth has been observed from the domestic investors, being the largest contributors than ever before. Moreover, as the interest rates become unattractive the investors gradually started shifting their investment avenues.

The investment in Mutual Fund is one of the growing areas of concern in the world of Investment Avenue. Basically investment in mutual fund is governed by its rate of return and the type of choice in the schemes provided. Simultaneously the behavioral aspects of the investors can also never be under emphasized. Hence rationale for selection of analysis regarding the returns of various schemes over a specific span has been stated in the chapter.

Mutual fund is a mechanism for pooling the resources by issuing units to the investors and investing funds in securities in accordance with the objectives as disclosed in offer document. Investments in securities are spread across a wide cross-section of industries and sectors and thus the risk is reduced. Diversification reduces the risk because all stocks may not move in the same direction in the same proportion at the same time.

The mutual funds normally come out with a number of schemes with different investment objectives which are launched from time to time. A mutual fund is required to be registered with Securities and Exchange Board of India (SEBI) which regulates securities markets before it can collect funds from the public. Thus mutual funds make saving and investing simple, accessible and affordable. The advantages of mutual funds include professional management, diversification, variety, liquidity, affordability, convenience, ease of recordkeeping, strict government regulation and full disclosures.

ADVANTAGES OF MUTUAL FUNDS

In early days of around 9,000 to 500 B.C. people used to invest their savings in livestock as cows and sheep, agricultural products as grain and vegetables and precious metal as silver and gold and land. That is, these were the traditional means of investment. In those days, investment was mainly for the purpose of preserving the money. Revolution in investment took place in 20th century with the introduction of banking system with many investment options as fixed deposits, post office savings, national saving certificate and bonds.

These options would serve the dual purpose i.e., provide returns as well as preserve the principal. The modern concept of investment states that any form of investment carries some degree of risk with it. Today many modern means of investment are available to the investors. Some of them carry low risk and low returns such as bank fixed deposits, national saving certificates, government securities, public provident fund etc. Some are high risk high return investment options such as commodity market, real estate, stock markets and mutual funds. These investment options provide different risk-return trade off catering to different types of needs of investors.

Mutual Funds have emerged as one of best investment options for all kinds of investors, whether their option is regular income or wealth accumulation. Mutual funds foster the buying power of an investors, so as to hold a large number of securities with a minimal investment, by reducing their risk. the following are the benefits of investing in Mutual funds.

1. **Diversification: -** The Fund Manager invests the pool of money in variety of assets like equities, bonds and money market instruments, so the risk of the portfolio is spread. If one type of asset class fails to generate returns, the returns from other assets will composite for the loss. The investors are less likely to lose their money invested. Diversification helps to reduce the risk of a portfolio. The fund manager assumes that "All eggs are not in the same basket".
2. **Highly Regulated: -** The investors are assumed that their invested is safe and it's been protected by the rules and regulations laid down by SEBI for the mutual fund industry. The regulations are designed to protect the investors interest. Association of Mutual Funds of India, a self-regulatory body has also issued guidelines with reference to NFO process, distributors, advertising and selling ethics also.
3. **Professional Management: -** When an investor chooses the mutual funds as their investment option, they also choosing the best professional managers. These fund managers take the decision of selecting the stocks for investment based on adequate

research. The fund manager is professionally qualified, experienced and are well aware about the capital market's status. Therefore, the investors get the benefit of earning wealth and regular returns through professional management of funds. The investor is relaxed, as the fund manager will review the portfolio whenever required.

4. **High Liquidity:** - Liquidity basically refers to the ability of asset converting into cash. Mutual funds are liquid in nature, as the investors can sell the fund units at the NAV on the given date and recover the money. Therefore, the money can be moved from the market in and out easily.
5. **Economies of Scale:** - As the mutual funds buys and sells the securities in large numbers, the transaction cost per unit get reduces. The retail investors with a small amount cannot afford themselves.
6. **Transparency:** - The mutual fund investment is quite transparent. All the companies are bound to follow the rules and regulations laid down by SEBI. The NAV's of the funds are updated by the companies on daily basis.
7. **Systematic approach to investment:** - The mutual funds offer variety of modes of investment to the investors. The investors can invest the money in mutual funds as per their convenience. They can either opt for lump sum, Systematic Investment Plan, Systematic Withdrawal Plans or Systematic Transfer Plan to switch from one fund to other. The investor can also opt for regular dividends or reinvestment (growth option).
8. **Tax Benefits:** - A special category of fund schemes such as equity linked savings schemes gives the tax benefit to the investors, by reducing their tax burden.
9. **Higher Returns:** - Mutual Funds are specially designed for the investors who can invest the money for a longer tenure. Longer the time period, larger will be the benefit of compounding.
10. **Variety of Products:** - Mutual fund industry offers a diverse range of mutual funds a scheme which satisfies the need of investors financial goals. The schemes also carrier different level

of risk suiting to the risk appetite of the investors. Different funds like equity, balanced, income, liquid, sectoral & money market mutual funds are available in the market.

11. **Smaller ticket size:** - The mutual funds work by pooling the money from investors and investing it in different securities. The investors can start with an investment as small as Rs. 100 per month, with systematic investment plan. The investors do not require huge corpus or capital to invest in mutual funds.
12. **Providing access to inaccessible securities:** - For a retail investor, it is almost impossible to invest the money in foreign stocks, international markets and bonds. But by investing in mutual funds the investor gets an opportunity to be part in ownership of these securities.
13. **Investment Comfort**: - Once the investor invests in mutual funds, they can make further investments in future just with a little documentation.

DISADVANTAGES OF MUTUAL FUNDS

In spite of having a large number of advantages, mutual funds also suffer from some serious limitations. Considering the fact that a large number of mutual funds are available in the market, but it is also very important for an investor to select the right scheme to their suiting their financial goals. Also, they have to bear the expense charges for the professional services they get. The following are the probable disadvantages of mutual fund investment.

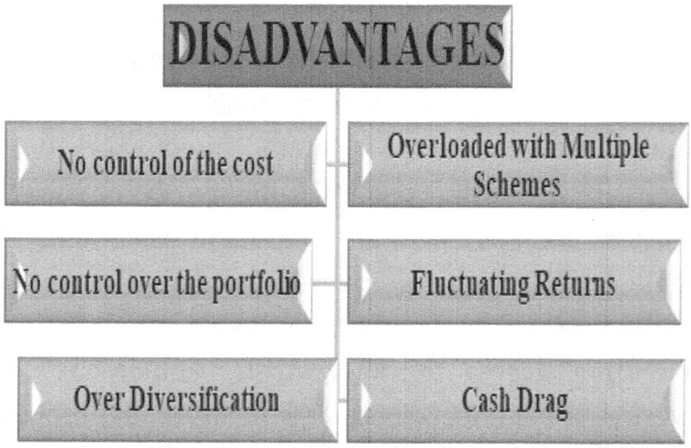

1. **No control of the Cost:** -The cost incurred by a scheme is been proportionately divided amongst the shareholders. Therefore, the investors do not have any control over the limit of cost to be incurred. As the expense ratio directly reduces the gains from mutual funds, it becomes a great concern for the investors.
2. **No control over the portfolio:** - The mutual fund investors do not have any control of which securities to be added in the portfolio to what percentage. However, large investors to get the benefit of Portfolio Management Schemes (PMS) to get a customized portfolio, but not all the investors get this service.
3. **Overloaded with multiple schemes:** - A variety of mutual fund schemes are floated in the market in huge numbers with a different investment objective. The investors get confused as to select which scheme for fulfilling their financial goals, and they need to seek the help of professional advisors.
4. **Fluctuating returns:** - Mutual funds are also subject to various risks, which will have a negative impact on the returns of the funds. Therefore, Mutual funds fail to offer fixed and guaranteed returns on investment.
5. **Over- Diversification of Portfolio:** One of the main advantages of mutual is diversification, overdiversification of the portfolio can also affect the investors adversely. If an investor holds a large number of securities in the portfolio, the

lesser are his chance to get individual returns. It reduces the risk on one hand but also decreases the chances of potential gain on selected good stocks.

6. **Cash Drag:** The AMC's have to maintain the large of amount in cash, to accommodate the liquidity demands of the investors. Therefore, a large amount of assets is maintained in cash by the mutual fund companies, which results in losing the gains on blocked up funds.

What Makes Mutual Funds Good Investment Options ?

Mutual funds are one of the most highly utilized investment options among average investors and financial professionals alike. But why is investing in a mutual fund a good idea? While some mutual funds are objectively better investment than others (and even others that serve very specific investment needs), what mutual funds grant investors access to is perhaps the most important benefit.

Mutual funds give investors the ability to diversify across a wide variety of investments that they otherwise may not carry in their portfolio as individual securities. Since mutual funds invest in a diverse range of securities and investment options, one mutual fund share actually represents proportionate ownership in each and every investment in the mutual fund's portfolio. Of most interest to investors is that each share also proportionately represents the profits of those investments as mutual funds are required to pass along profits to their investors by way of mutual fund distributions, which come in several forms.

In a mutual fund, the value of your shares goes up and down as the value of the stocks and bonds in the fund rise and fall. For the average investor to have the same exposure to those investment options and potential profits on their own would be extremely costly both in terms of the actual investment dollars and in terms of time.

Additionally, investing in a mutual fund is generally a cost-effective way to gain access to professional money management. Were you to try and invest in individual securities and actively manage them the way a mutual fund's manager does; it could very easily become a full-time job? In order to make wise investment decisions when you buy individual stocks and bonds yourself, at the very least you'd have to have the knowledge to do extensive research on various types of businesses in general (automobile, construction, medical) and on specific companies (GE, IBM, Microsoft).

This is work that most of us are not interested in, do not have the time for, and, most importantly, are probably not as qualified to do. By purchasing shares of a mutual fund, you're also purchasing the money management and investment skills of the fund manager whose job it is to invest and reinvest the mutual fund's capital based on the fund's established goals.

Chapter 2

Types of Mutual Funds

A variety of mutual fund schemes with different and unique investment objectives are floated in the market to fulfil the financial needs of the investors. These schemes are discussed on detail as below:

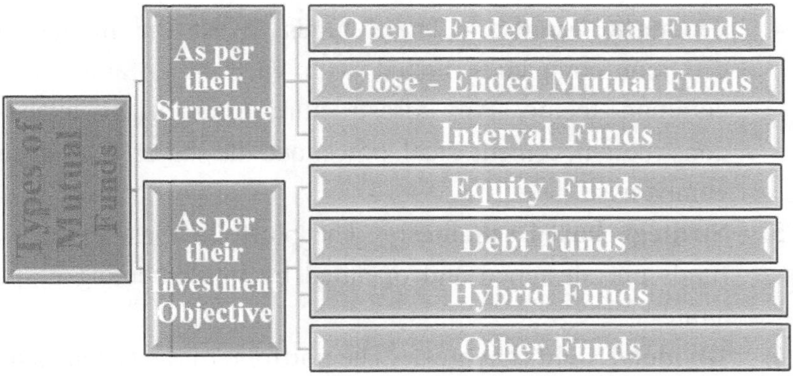

1. **Open ended Schemes:** - There funds give the liability to the investors to enter or exit the scheme even after NFO. The units are bought and sold in the market at the NAV. This provides liquidity to the investors as well as switching across the schemes also becomes easy.
2. **Close ended Schemes:** - The funds have a fixed maturity. The units of the scheme can only be purchased during the NFO process. A close ended fund raises the capital only once through an NFO. The listing of close ended funds on stock exchange is compulsory.

❖ **EQUITY FUNDS**

1. **Diversified Equity Fund: -** These types of funds invest the money in diverse range of securities to reduce the risk of the scheme. The poor returns of one stock will be compensated by other stocks performing better.
2. **Market Segment based Funds: -** The mutual fund companies invest the pooled money in securities on the basis of its market size. Large Cap Funds, Mid Cap Funds, Small Cap Funds and Multi Cap Funds.
3. **Sector Funds: -** The mutual funds schemes invest only in a specific sector. For example, A Pharma Fund will invest only in the shares of pharmaceutical companies. The performance of the scheme is linked with the performance of that specific sector. The scheme is more likely to carry more risk than other equity schemes.
4. **Thematic Funds: -** These funds invest the money across different companies linked with each other and are under common theme. An infrastructure fund might invest into construction, cement, steel, power and the shares of other related companies.
5. **Strategy based schemes: -** The portfolio these categories of funds one designed and operated by implementing a specific strategy.
6. **Dividend yield schemes: -** The portfolio of the schemes invests in the companies which have stable returns and growth. The NAV of these schemes do not fluctuate more as compared to other schemes.
7. **Value Funds: -** These funds are generally preferred by the investors whose goal is capital appreciation. The fund manager identifies the companies which are financially strong firms, but currently their shares must not be performing well, but expectations are there of their recovering with higher market values.
8. **Focused Funds: -** There funds only invest in limited number of securities. They only focus on the stocks of 25-30 companies;

therefore, it is also known as "concentrated fund". The fund manager has been very careful in picking up the right stocks for the portfolio.

9. **ELSS (Equity Linked Savings Scheme): -** The funds offer tax benefits to the investors under section 80C. These schemes invest up to 75% to 80% of money in equity schemes but have a lock in period of 3 years. During this tenure the investor can't transfer, switch or redeem the mutual fund units.

DEBT FUNDS

These funds basically invest in debt securities such as PSU and Government Bonds. These schemes are basically preferred by the investors having a lower risk appetite. They are categorized as below:

On the basis of Issuer: -

1. **Gilt Funds: -** These funds only invest in those securities which carrier almost no risk or we can say are risk free, such as treasury bills, commercial papers, and government securities. These funds are highly liquid and carries a minimal amount of risk. Moreover, these funds also generate lower returns to the investors but are highly safe.
2. **Corporate bond Funds: -** The portfolios of these funds specifically invest in the public sector and private sector bonds. These funds carry higher credit risk, as the price of the bond gets affected by the interest rate changes.

On the basis of Tenure: -

1. **Liquid Schemes: -** These debt schemes invest only in the securities having a maturity up to 91 days. The securities which have a maturity period exceeding 60 days are valued are "Mark to Market". The investors who have low risk appetite and only focuses on safety of principle will prefer these funds.
2. **Short Term debt Funds: -** The portfolios of these funds invest in low risk and ultra-short-term debt securities.

3. **Long Term debt Schemes:** - These schemes invest in long term debt securities likes bonds issued by public and private sector. The return of these schemes is also not stable, as the value of securities fluctuates.

On the basis of Investment Style: -

1. **Income Funds:** - These schemes portfolio comprises of a judicious mix of debt securities by government and non-government. The corporate bonds assets in giving higher yields while the government securities offer liquidity to the investors.
2. **Junk bond Schemes:** - These schemes invest the money in bonds of the companies which have a pool credit rating. The bonds have huge credit risk but can generate good profits as well.
3. **Fixed Maturity Plans:** - The investment in these plans can only be made at the time of new fund offer. It has a fixed maturity period which ranges between 30 days to 5 years. The investors get protection from the market fluctuations.
4. **Floating rate Funds:** - These funds invest in financial securities that pay a variable return. For example, "A 5-year bond plus 1% will pay 7% interest. If the actual interest rate is 6%".

HYBRID FUNDS

These categories of funds invest in different asset class like equity, debt and government securities. The percentage of assets in the portfolio will depend upon the investment objective. If the equity content is higher the risk will be higher and if the debt content is higher than will carry a lesser risk.

1. **Equity oriented Hybrid Funds:** - These schemes invest a major part of its money into equity funds which will generate capital appreciation and a smaller debt content to bring stability in returns.
2. **Debt oriented Hybrid Funds:** - The portfolio of these funds highly comprises of debt securities and only a very little

proportion of equity. The proportion of equity can be also as low as 5%, to avoid the variability in returns.

3. **Capital protection Schemes:** - The aim of these funds to provide the safety of principle amount to the investors. These funds basically invest in zero coupon government securities which carries very less credit risk. The schemes fundamentally assume the principal amount back, despite of the market fluctuations.
4. **Arbitrage Funds:** - These funds invest not only in different securities but also in different markets, so as to minimize the risk and earn good returns. A fund purchased in NSE and selling the shame in BSE parallel at higher price with generate good returns to shareholders.

SOLUTION ORIENTED SCHEMES

1. **Retirement Fund:** - This fund is aimed at providing retirement benefits to the investors. These schemes have a lock in period of 5 years of retirement age which is earlier.
2. **Children's Fund:** - These funds are specially designed for helping kids in attainment of children's dream. These funds also come with a specified lock in period.

OTHER SCHEMES

1. **Funds of Funds**: - The particular schemes of mutual fund invest their money in other schemes of mutual funds. The investor gets an advantage of investing in different mutual fund schemes at one go. The schemes may choose all the funds from the same AMC or different AMC's depending upon the objective.
2. **Emerging Market Funds:** - This fund invests the money in the developing economies around the world. The developing and emerging economies will contribute the overall global growth in future to a larger extent.
3. **International / Foreign Funds:** The investment of these funds is spread in the stocks and assets of different countries. These

funds either invest its entire funds in international securities or can divide the investment by investing some amount in Indian securities and some in foreign stocks.

INVESTMENT STYLES IN MUTUAL FUNDS

Discipline in Investment is imperative for investors to increase their returns on investment. Mutual Fund offers systematic ways of investing and redeeming the money from mutual funds, which covers the following.

1. **Systematic Investment Plan (SIP):** - This approach of investing in mutual funds states that a field time interval in a selected mutual funds scheme. The time interval usually is monthly. This approach of investment is considered as one of the best methods to yield higher returns on investments. Investors will land in getting more units, when the markets are low. This leads to high returns when market recovers. A SIP helps an investor to maintain an average price during its investment tenure. In the recent times SIP has become the most popular method of investing in mutual funds for the retail investors, the investment in an SIP starts at a very nominal rate i.e. 100 even. It not only offers a systematic investment but also flexibility to the small retail investors. It helps the investors to participate in the capital market with a minimal amount and build up the wealth at a longer period of time. It helps the small investors to make big money as SIP investment id based in the rupee cost averaging method.

SIP – The Unique tool of Wealth Creation:

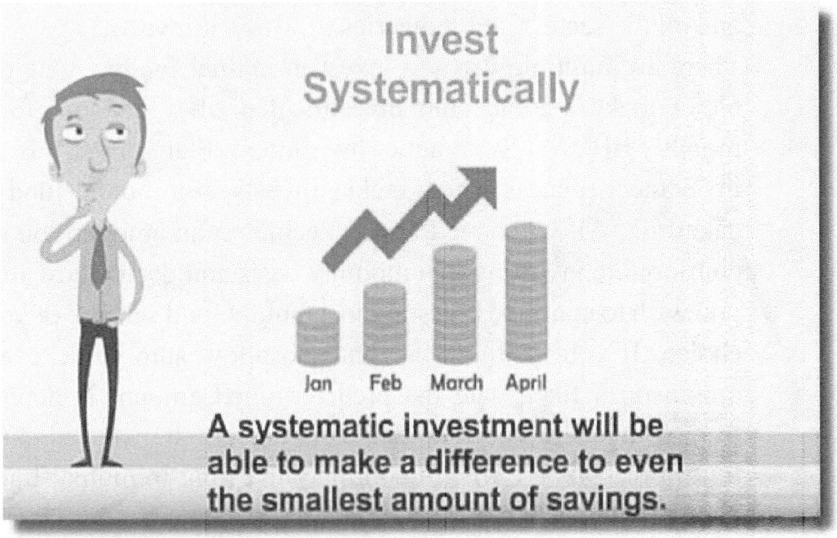

1. If you are wondering how to grow you existing wealth, financial planning should be your primary focus. It is impossible to multiply your existing wealth by letting it sit alone in the bank. When you know your short term and long-term financial goals, you might be able to come up with an investment plan that is more apt for your income needs. Those who are risk averse, such individuals usually have a tough time finding the right scheme. With falling interest rates, one can hardly expect conservative schemes to help them achieve their life's long term financial goals.
2. If you are a young individual with an appetite for risk who is seeking long term capital appreciation by investing in a market linked scheme and keen on adding an aggressive touch to their investment strategy, you can consider investing in mutual funds. A mutual fund is an investment vehicle for pooling from investors and collectively investing the capital raised to achieve a common investment objective. Mutual fund managers must buy / sell securities in accordance with the asset allocation strategy and investment strategy to help the scheme outperform its underlying benchmark. The performance of a mutual fund

scheme depends on the performance of its underlying assets and all the sectors and industries in which it invests.

3. There are multiple ways to invest in mutual funds – One can either make a lump sum investment or they can opt for a monthly **SIP**. A Systematic Investment Plan or SIP is an investment process which makes investing in mutual funds a cakewalk. All you have to do is decide on an amount you are comfortable investing in a monthly basis and decide how long you wish to continue investing in a mutual fund scheme of your choice. If you instruct your bank to allow auto debit, every month on a fixed date the predetermined amount is debited from your savings account and electronically transferred to the fund. Investors are free to continue investing in mutual funds via SIP till their investment objective is achieved.

How do SIPs work?

A SIP enables you to break your investments over a quarterly or a monthly period. One can either give post-dated cheques or easily opt for the electronic clearing service (ECS) under which your bank will automatically debit the given amount on a specific date, to be invested in the mutual fund scheme.

SIPs are ideal for investors who don't have the market expertise, a big lump sum to be invested immediately or the time to constantly monitor their investments. Through SIPs, you can easily apply the power of compounding on your investments and build a sizeable corpus over time.

Benefits of SIPs

SIPs reduce risk by Rupee Cost Averaging

When you invest using the SIP option, you buy units at different net asset values (NAVs). For example, if the market is going higher, the NAV will be more, resulting in lesser units as compared to when market is down, where you will end up buying more units.

Hence SIPs help you to ride market volatility in a profitable way by automatically buying more when the prices are falling and less when they are rising. This also lowers the average purchase price for your investment as seen in rupee cost averaging.

SIPs can be started with as little as Rs 500 each month. SIPs provide flexibility in choosing the amount you want to invest and you can choose your frequency as daily/weekly/fortnightly or monthly. SIPs make it easy to achieve long-term financial goals as your investments are broken down into smaller, less daunting, regular investments.

SIPs also offer freedom from being on the constant look out for opportunities to time the market. Over the long-term, the ups and downs of the market get evened out.

One of the key advantages of investing through SIPs is that they inculcate financial discipline making you invest a fixed amount consistently at regular intervals. By starting early, even with a small amount, you can build a sizeable corpus to achieve your financial goals.

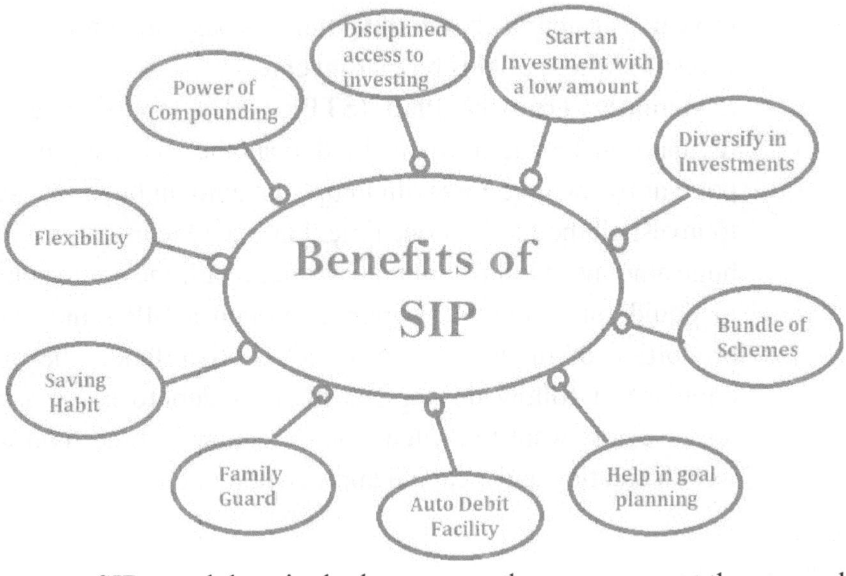

SIPs work best in the long run as they average out the ups and downs of the stock market, prevent you from taking detrimental decisions based on emotions and offer better potential returns. As a wise investor, you should leverage the benefit of SIPs as a means to invest bit by bit and achieve the investment goal that you have in mind.

Benefits of SIP as compare to Lump Sum investment

- You don't need to speculate or focus on timing the market (which isn't the right way for generating returns over long term)
- Amount is invested on monthly basis, so there is little to no impact of market volatility (unit cost averaging)
- Passive and automated (monthly installments can be deducted automatically) approach makes you more committed to guaranteed saving/investment
- It's very flexible - you can create/update/cancel SIP anytime. Most of the funds starts as low as Rs. 1000 per month

4. **Systematic Withdrawal Plans: -** SWP refers to regular redemption of fixed amount from a mutual fund. The investor can also opt for either fixed amount redemption or a fixed unit's resumption or a fixed unit's redemption every month, quarter or year. The approach of mutual funds is basically preferred by investors whose goal is regular income.
5. **Systematic Transfer Plan (STP): -** The option refers to regular transferring from one fund to another. This approach is popular by the investors with lump sum amount but don't want to invest all the funds at one time. For e.g. One investor with a huge amount of lump sum money might park the entire sum in in liquid fund, and every month through a SIP same Fixed proportion of funds are transferred to other fund. The most popular STP followed is transferring from debt to equity, when the investors want to switch from a regular income fund to a wealth creation and a capital appreciation one.

Chapter 3

Legal Structure of Mutual Fund in India

The role of SEBI is to protect interest of the investors as well as to regulate the Capital Market. SEBI has issued guidelines and polices, for the AMC's, Intermediaries, and the investors from time to time, so as to ensure the growth of the financial market as well. SEBI suggests that a firm must first configure an Asset Management Company for starting up the mutual fund business.

The key Features of Mutual Fund are as below

✓ It is a trust

✓ It pools the savings from Investors

✓ The funds are having different schemes as per the people's financial needs

✓ It invests the money in a wide range of securities, gold and even real estate.

SEBI being the regulator and controller of mutual funds have prescribed the legal structure for the Indian Mutual Funds industry. It includes the following aspects.

1. Mutual Funds are trusts and are managed by Indian Trusts Act 1882.
2. Mutual Funds works through a four-tier structure, which includes custodian, AMC, Trustees and Sponsor.
3. The Trust is been created by the Sponsors.
4. The beneficiaries of mutual funds are its investors.

5. The trust is guided by the trustees. Who's aimed to protect the interest of its investors.
6. The mutual funds trust is administered by a trust deed.
7. The routine functions and the management of the schemes is performed by an Asset Management Company, which is appointed by the trustees.
8. The trustees appoint a custodian which maintains the custody of the assets held by AMC.
9. The records of transactions of various Mutual Fund Schemes are maintained by registrar and transfer agents

MAJOR CONSTITUENTS OF MUTUAL FUNDS

1. **Sponsors:** - Sponsors are the one who apply to SEBI for mutual fund and are considered to be a backbone of the fund is organization. They contribute at least 40% of their capital in AMC, as well having a financial services experience of 5 years or more.
2. **Trustee:** - The trustees have to perform a pivotal role in ensuring that the fund is following all the legal compliances, rules and regulations laid down by SEBI. Approval of SEBI is must for an appointing trustee. 4 trustees have to be appointed by the sponsor.
3. **AMC:** - An AMC is responsible for smooth day to day operations of mutual funds, which includes infrastructure, employees, sales & promotion, software and to maintain healthy relation with service providers. AMC is required to have a minimum net worth of 50 crores. AMC have to ensure due diligence in its investment style. An AMC can also be terminated by 75% of unit holders. The trustee can also terminate the AMC.
4. **Custodian:** - All the custodians are appointed by the trustees and have to compulsorily register under SEBI. The role of a custodian is settling the transactions on behalf of mutual funds. The custodian accepts and give the delivery for the purchase and sole of stocks.

5. **Registrar and Transfer Agents:** - RTA's are also appointed by AMC. AMC can perform these activities themselves, but they appoint RTA's for their convenience to get the records of mutual funds. RTA's maintains the data of transactions, cancellation, issuing certificates and solving the investors issues.

HISTORY OF MUTUAL FUNDS

The most popular investment avenue "Mutual Fund" was established way back in 1772-73 in Dutch Republic by a businessman Abraham. He created a trust to provide small investors good returns in the time of financial crisis. These investment funds also were launched in 1849 in Switzerland and in Scotland in 1880's.

However, formally mutual funds were introduced in 1924 in U.S.A. These funds were basically close ended in nature. Massachusetts Investors trust introduced the first open ended mutual funds schemes in 1924. Back then, close ended schemes were more popular than the open-ended schemes. The growth of the mutual fund industry increased at a higher pace from 1950's after the introduction of money market mutual funds and Index funds.

The institutional and the retail investors had started showing the interest in mutual funds. The number of mutual funds. The number of mutual funds in U.S.A. reflected a humongous growth just from a 70 funds in 1940 to around 3000 funds in 1989, which shows the increasing popularity of mutual funds. Mutual funds also started gaining popularity in Europe, Australia, Latin America, Canada and Asian Countries as well. However, surprisingly countries like Japan, UK, Germany reflected a growth of 300 to 500%.

Earlier till 1989's mutual funds were not much popular among the retail investors, but since the start of 1990's they had also started considering mutual funds as a popular investment option. Mutual fund industry stood second amongst the financial services sector, banking still being the first in 1995.As per the study by Laderman and Smith (1993). The investment in equity shares almost doubled by 96% in 1993, because of the investment by Mutual Funds. The uniform regulatory policy in case of investment, disclosure and structure also boosted up the popularity of mutual funds in Asia-pacific region, including Thailand, Hong Kong and Korea.

DEVELOPMENT OF MUTUAL FUND INDUSTRY IN INDIA

The mutual fund industry in India has grown leaps and bounds in the past two decades and has come a long way since the introduction of mutual funds in India for the first time in 1963.

The industry has shown an exceptional growth in terms of AUM, number of schemes, number of AMC's and the most important being the number of investors. The Indian Mutual Fund industry has also faced a lot of challenges to be on the position, where it is today. The mutual fund industry was established in the year 1963 and its growth is reflected in different phases.

A. Phase 1(1964-1987) Ruled by UTI: -

During this period UTI was the only sole player in the Indian Mutual Fund industry. UTI was established in 1963, which was set up by RBI. The first mutual fund scheme was launched by UTI in 1964, named US-64. It was the first open ended and popular mutual fund scheme till date. The assets of these schemes showed an outstanding increase from 49 crores in 1965 to 219 crores in 1987. UTI launched its first ever growth scheme named "Master Share" in 1986, and also one foreign scheme listed on London Stock Exchange. At the end of this phase UTI managed to accumulate 6700 crores as its AUM.

B. Phase 2 (1987-1993) Arrival of Public Sector Funds: -

During this phase the government permitted banks, insurance companies and financial institutions to enter the MF industry in 1987 due to new government policy. SBI launched the first public sector funds which initiated by a bank in 1987. The phase witnessed an entry of 8 new mutual funds including one by LIC in 1989 and by GIC in 1990, by insurance companies. Not only the degree of competition increased but, the fund mobilization and total AUM of the industry also witnessed a tremendous growth. The total AUM increased up to 47004 crores in 1993, by the end of this phase.

C. Phase 3 (1993-2003) Entry of Private Players:

The golden period of Mutual Fund Industry started with the entry of private sector funds and SEBI came up more detailed, revised and strict guidelines for the operations of mutual funds. So as to protect the investors interest and maintain transparency. Association of Mutual Funds in India – a self-regulatory body was also established in the year 1995, which an aim of promoting mutual funds, and spreading awareness amongst the investors. In 1993, the first private sector fund "Kothari Pioneer Fund" was floated in the market. Till 1995, a total of 11 private funds was issued.

The entry of private funds also brought a tremendous change in the industry with reference of product innovation, investors services, product structure and design and information disclosure. Because of this, the industry has shown a growth in terms of number of schemes & AUM. The turning point of this phase was an announcement in budget 1999, that the dividend income from mutual funds were fully exempted in the hands of investors.

The acquisition of Pioneer Mutual Fund by Templeton, a multinational firm was a decisive moment of the Mutual Fund Industry. The total AUM at the end of this phase had crossed a mark of one trillion in 2003, which was an achievement in itself.

D. Phase 4 (Since 2003): -

This phase in February 2003 has witnessed a bifurcation of UTI, the oldest and the first mutual fund in to two separate entities. The first entity "UTI Specified undertaking" was regulated by Indian Government, and the other "ÜTI Mutual Fund limited" was registered and controlled by SEBI. The second entity was sponsored by public sector player namely SBI, PNB, Bank of Baroda and LIC. During this phase a lot of International companies also entered the market, which resulted in merger and acquisitions of fund houses. The Mutual Fund industry reached one landmark by reaching an AUM of 3 trillion in 2006. By the end of this phase the assets raised to 417300 crores in March 2009. During this phase the industry has also went through a major revolutionary change in terms of the number of mergers and acquisitions. A number of bold steps were also taken by SEBI, to pump in more money in to the market by eliminating the entry load.

KEY DOCUMENTS TERMINOLOGY FOR MUTUAL FUNDS

1. **NFO (New Fund Offer):** - The mutual funds units are floated in market for the investors first time through an NFO. The decision of NFO is taken on the basis of suggestions given by Chief Investment Officer and Chief Marketing Officer. AMC takes the call, as what time the scheme should be introduced in the market. All NFO's other then ELSS remains open for the purpose of purchase for 15 days.
2. **Offer Document**: - The AMC have to prepare a offer document to launch a NFO. The offer document contains all the minute details about the schemes. It is the most important document which contains all the legal and fundamental details about the scheme. The disclosure details are also prescribed by SEBI. It includes

➢ Type of Scheme i.e., open ended or close ended and Equity/Debt or Hybrid
➢ Investment objective
➢ Investment Pattern
➢ Provisions of listing, Purchase & Sale
➢ Fees Charged

3. **SID (Scheme Information Document):** - SID is a part of offer document. It covers the details like number of units offered its face value, nature of scheme, NFO opening and Closing Date, and the details of AMC issuing the scheme. Moreover, it also covers details such as risk factor, due diligence certificate, expense ratio, load charges and penalties. This particular document can be referred by the investors for 21 days on the website of SEBI. SID document has to update every year.
4. **SAI (Scheme Additional Information):** - This is also a part of offer document, which covers the managerial details of the scheme. It contains details about the AMC, Trustees, Sponsors,

Custodian, Registrar and Transfer Agents, Bankers and Accountants. SAI have to have updated at end of every quarter. Furthermore, the information about the number of schemes launched by the AMC and its comparative performance is also been disclosed in SAI.

5. **KIM (Key Information Memorandum)**: - The brief statement which contains the details of both SID and SAI is known as KIM. This document is easily available in the market and it is been widely used by the investors. Basically, this document covers all the key points necessary to be considered before making an investment. KIM is attached with every application. KIM is also updated once a year.

SIGNIFICANT TERMINOLOGY OF MUTUAL FUNDS INVESTMENT

1. **NAV: -** Net Asset Value represent the market value of the mutual fund scheme on a specified date. NAV for a mutual scheme is calculated at the end of each trading day. The NAV value is useful to the investors, researchers and fund managers to be value of mutual fund. Depending on the performance of mutual fund i.e. the stocks and securities, the NAV of a fund may be high or low. NAV is the net different between the assets held and the liabilities by a fund.

   NAV = Net Assets of the Fund / Number of units outstanding

2. **Load Charges: -** Load refers to that amount which is deducted by the AMC's at the time of redemption of scheme. This fee is been levied from the investors for discoursing them from the redemption. The percentage of load depends on the tenure of investment and the type of scheme and it is decided by individual AMC. Load charges are levied on redemption of funds it the redemption of investment is less than a year. However, the entry load on investment has been removed by SEBI in August 2009.

3. **Expense Ratio: -** This ration reflects all operational and managerial expenses incurred to run the fund. Expense ratio basically covers management fees, Administrative costs and 12-1b distribution fees. The fees are the compensation as the AMC manager and operators the funds well and also generate good returns. Expense ratios of ETF's are lower as compared to other schemes. If the Assets of the funds are lesser in size than the expense ratio will be high. On other hand as the assets held by the funds increases the expense will reduce.

ROLE OF MUTUAL FUND CONTROLLERS & REGULATORS

1. Securities and Exchange Board of India (SEBI)

SEBI mutual funds regulations were laid down in the year 1996. As mutual funds have become an important driving force of the Indian Capital Market, SEBI has laid down a comprehensive guideline regarding the issue, structure and framework of Mutual Funds. SEBI has laid down rules and regulations with reference for issue, transfer, redemption, disclosure of information and investor's protection. It regulates the trustees, AMC's, Sponsor's, Custodian's, RTA's, Banker's and the Broker's related with the operation of Mutual Funds. Recently SEBI have provided with the guidelines about the expense ratio and its limit. All the AMC's have to compulsorily follow the guidelines to keep the expense ratio under the prescribed limit, as that factor have a negative impact of the fund's NAV.

The brief guidelines are discussed as below:

- All mutual fund has to register themselves as Trusts under Indian Trust Act 1882.
- 80% of funds in case of ELSS should be invested in Equity Linked Stocks.
- AMC have to contribute 10 crores to run the business of Mutual Funds, where in 40% must be contributed by sponsors.
- Mutual Funds cannot enter into option or forward trading.

- AMC's can also provide services regarding conclusion-based schemes like pension schemes.
- Mutual funds have to only investment in transferable securities, but the investment in a single company should not exceed more than 15% of its total.
- Investment of funds in short-term deposits and banking securities should not exceed more than 15%.
- The custodian should be registered with the bond.
- An AMC with every close ended scheme needs to pool 20 crores, while for an open-ended scheme it should be 50 crores.
- AMC have to maintain proper records with reference to all managerial and operational expenses for operating a mutual fund.
- Mutual Fund will not give any loans.
- A SEBI authorized auditor will verify the records and audit the books of a mutual fund.
- All mutual funds have to follow uniform guidelines for issuing funds, calculating, NAV, redemption, valuation of securities and disclosure of information.
- Any MF scheme will only invest in listed securities.

2. Association of Mutual Funds in India

AMFI was established in the year 1995, with an objective to protect the investors interest. AMFI is a non-profit organization which is dedicated at building professional and ethical standards for the mutual fund industry in India. Presently all 44 AMC's are members of AMFI.

The main objectives of AMFI includes.

- Defining and maintaining high level of professional and ethical standards for the operations of Mutual Fund.
- Interaction with SEBI on all matters related to MF.
- To develop a well-trained professional team of Mutual Fund Distributors.

- To implant guidelines for the certification and training of MF Distributors.
- To arrange investors awareness programs, which will focus on the working and benefits of MF's to Investors.
- For circulation of the information about the mutual fund industry.
- To frame the standard of good practices which AMC's need to follow.

Chapter 4

Current Scenario of the Indian Mutual Fund Industry

The Indian MF industry has evolved and grown enormously and gigantically in the past two decades. The industry has overcome a lot of challenges and have managed to reach new milestones with reference to number of Asset Management Companies, Number of Schemes launched and the Assets under Management, and have witnessed a dramatic growth in the past 20 years. The Indian Mutual Fund Industry is in its transformation phase and is focused towards tapping the savings of retail investors by bring about a revolutionary change which in turn will be a boon for them.

With around 40 plus Asset Management Companies, more than 1500 active scheme's, in diverse areas like equity, debt, liquid, balance, gilt, ETF's and many more, the industry have a wide range of products to offer which are in tune with the financial goals of the investors. The AMC's, AMFI and SEBI are proactively working together for the better mechanism of the industry. On one hand a lot of regulatory changes are going on to ensure investors protection and satisfaction as well as on other hand mutual fund houses are restructuring their business models to improve their efficiencies.

The contribution of the Mutual Fund Industry in the economy and its growth can't be overlooked. The contribution is smaller as compared to the other developed nations, but a steady increase has been noticed in the past 10 years, which is tremendous. The ways and means by which SEBI, AMFI, AMC's and the players of the industry are promoting the mutual funds as key investment avenue for the individual investors through various investor awareness programs, advertisement campaigns and the social media is tremendous.

The share of investment in mutual funds has increased by 16% in last three years and on other hand the investment in bank deposits have fallen to 65% in March 2019 from 72% in March 2017. The mutual fund industry has been fast in adopting the regulations of SEBI, and therefore the Asset under Management has shown a sharp increase. The Average AUM of Indian Mutual Fund Industry in September 2020 has touched the landmark of 27.74 Lakh crores. The Total Assets was just 6.5 trillion in September 2010, while it stands to be 26.85 Trillion for September 2020, which reflects a notable and steep rise of AUM by 4 times in a decade.

Chart Showing Growth in the Total Assets during the COVID Pandemic

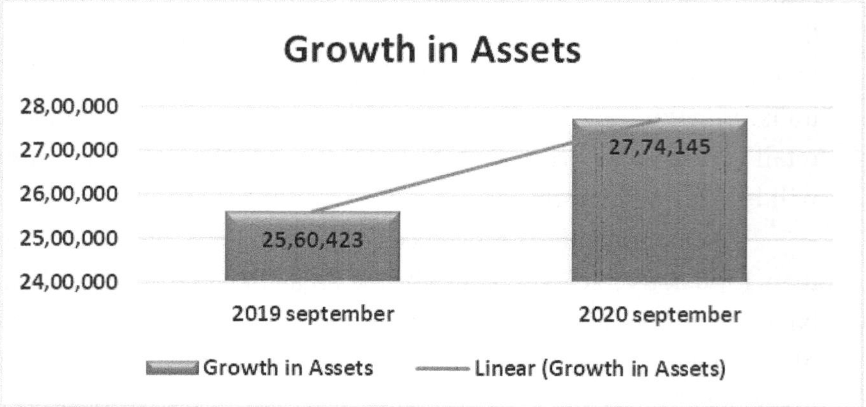

Source: AMFI **(Rs in Crores)**

The above chart reflects the total assets held by AMC's in September 2019 and 2020. COVID Pandemic have affected all the industries and spheres across the world, and Mutual Fund Industry is no different. However, to our utter surprise, the total assets have seen an exponential increase even during the Covid crisis. The above chart ponders that the total assets have increased by 8.35%.

The total assets in September 2019 were 25.60 trillion, which rose to 27.74 trillion in September 2020. This is a reflection of the belief of the investors in mutual funds. The Indian investors have preferred mutual funds as their investment avenue to park their finances even during the pandemic.

Chart Showing Total Assets from September 2019 to September 2020

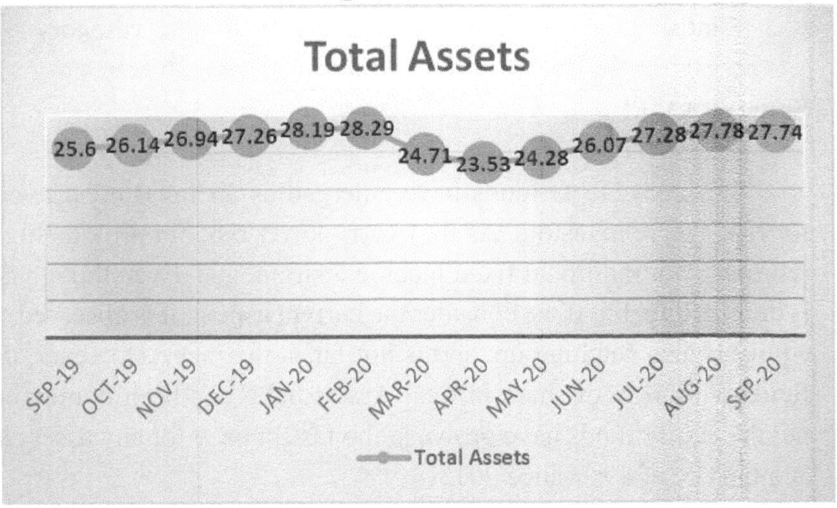

Source:AMFI **(in Trillions)**

The Mutual fund industry have witnessed a considerable and substantial growth in the past two decades. The industry has shown a surge rise in the total assets, number of accounts, average ticket size and number of schemes.

The above chart shows the total assets on monthly basis, from September 2019 to September 2020. There shows a drop in the total assets from the month March, April, and May 2020 due to the COVID effect. However, the industry has revitalized and bounced backed, as we can see that the total assets have started soaring again.

Chart Showing Breakup of Total AUM as on 31st March 2019

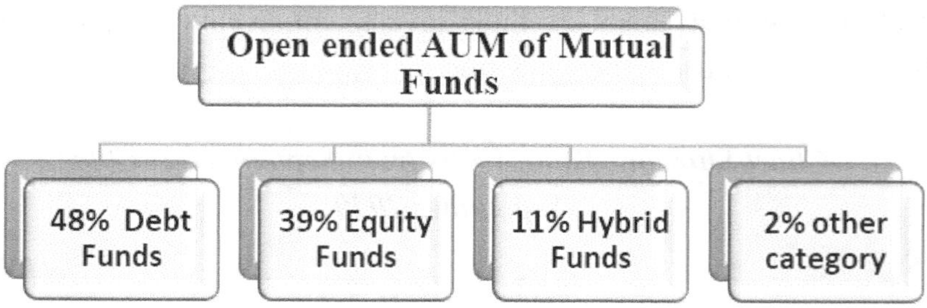

Source: AMFI

March Debts funds have emerged as an investment avenue for risk averse investors. As they carry lower risk but provide higher returns, than traditional fixed income instruments. Even though debt is dominating, but if we consider the current aspect, it is observed that equity is also catching up, and is not far in the race. However, debt funds with 48% of share in total Assets held, has been dominating, but the equity funds have grown at the fastest pace for any asset class at a CAGR of 49% since 2013.

Chart showing Constitution of Investors holding

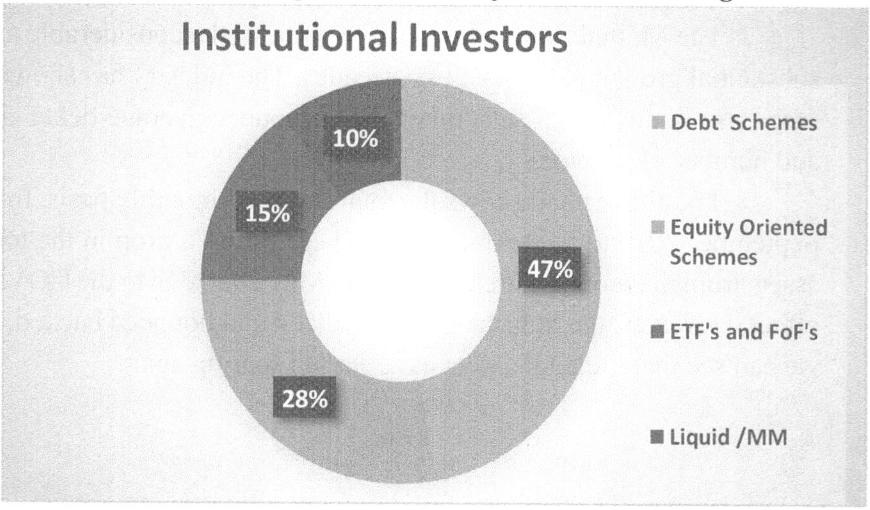

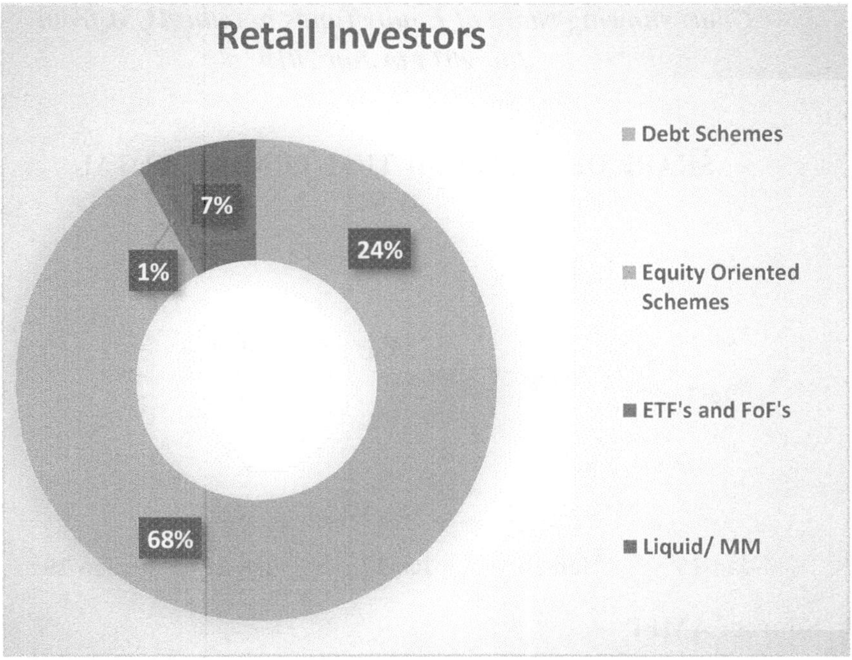

Source: AMFI

The above chart provides that with reference to the individual or retail investors, the major preference for investment is given to Equity oriented schemes, as these schemes are capable of not only providing dividends but having high probability of wealth creation.

The individual investors future goals are retirement planning, education, or marriage of their children; therefore, their first preference is equity schemes, followed by Debt Schemes and EFT's being the last choice. While on the other hand Institutional Investors prefer to invest their money in more safe and liquid investment vehicles, so their preference will be debt and balanced schemes.

Chart showing share of Equity funds in total AUM from Jan 2014 to Jan 2019

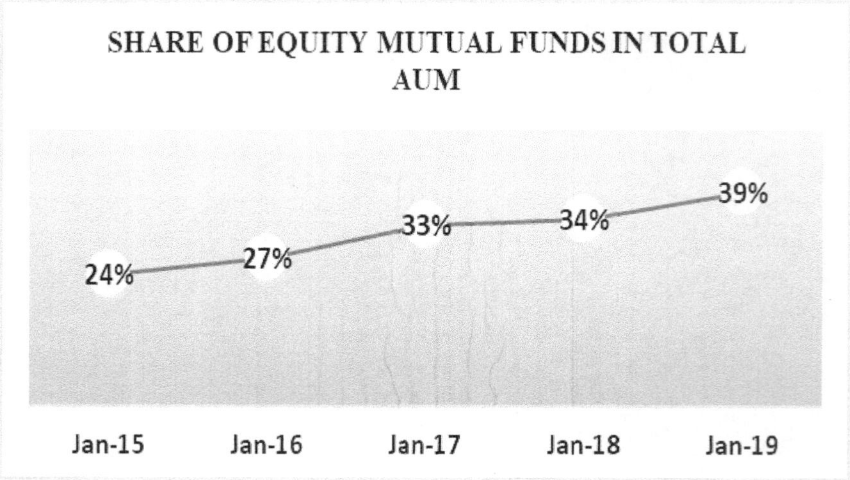

Source: AMFI

Mutual fund industry in India has majorly been dominated by the debt-oriented funds, followed by balanced schemes and then equity-oriented funds. However, looking at the trend, the picture seems to be changing. The share of equity-oriented schemes in the total sum of AUM was 23% in 2013, which escalated to 39% in 2019.

Percentage of Accounts Across Investor Types form September 2019 to 2020

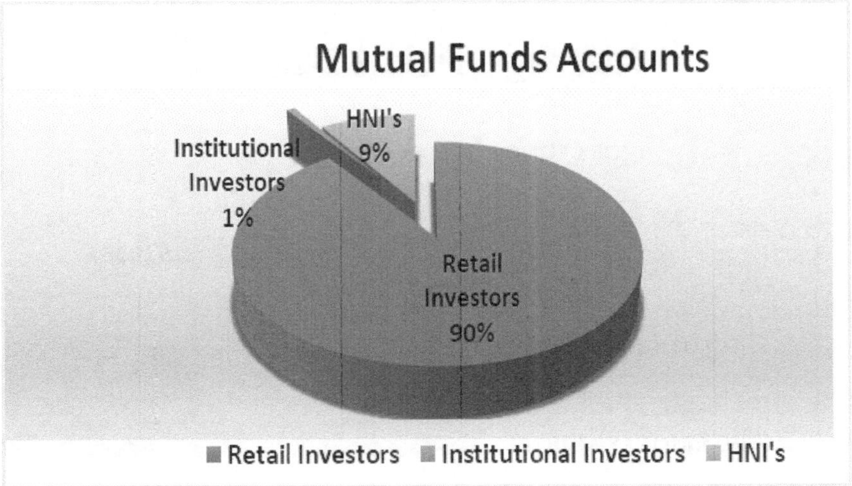

Source: AMFI

September 2020 has been one of the remarkable months for the Mutual Fund Industry in India. Out of the total accounts opened, 90% of accounts of Individual Investors, and just 1% of Institutional investors. The data reflects that the faith and the trust of retail investors is still in Mutual Funds for their investment.

Chart showing Average Ticket Size across the Mutual Fund schemes.

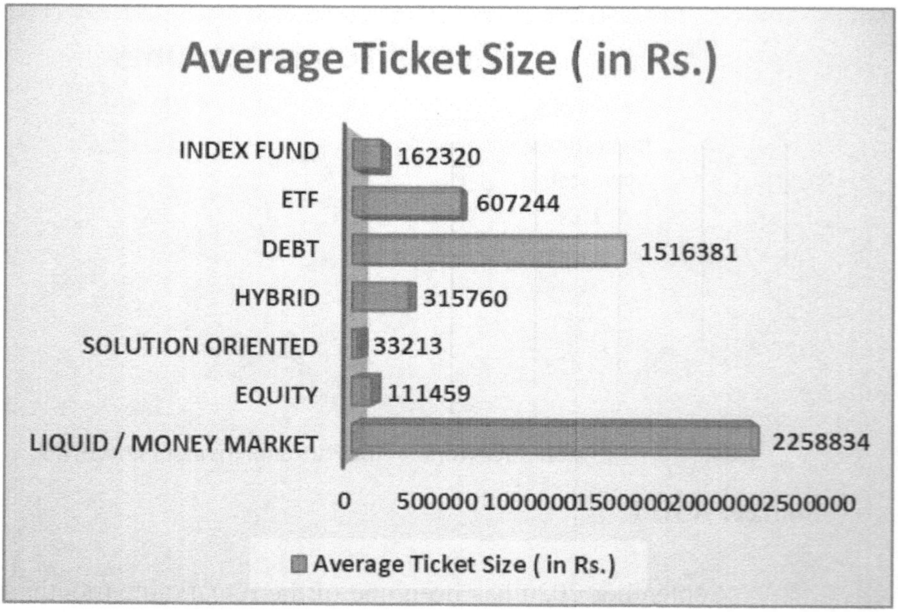

Source: AMFI

The average ticket size for Liquid and Money market Funds is the highest i.e. Rs.2258834, followed by Debt oriented schemes i.e. Rs.1516381, as these funds are popular with the institutional investors. Whereas the average ticket size for equity-oriented schemes is Rs. 111459, as this category is dominated by the individual investors.

Graph showing Average Ticket Size of Individual Investors from March 2010 to March 2019

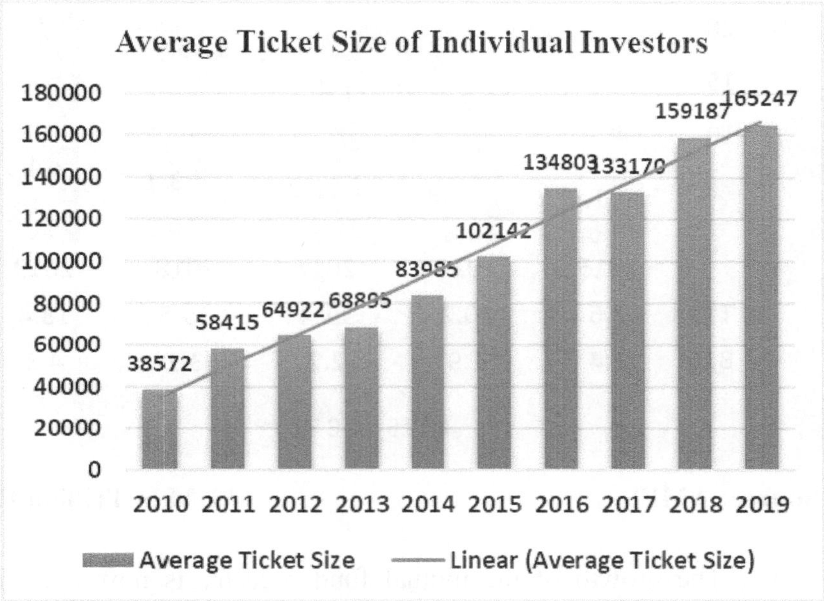

Source:AMFI **(Ticket Size in Rs)**

As per the recent analysis of the Indian Mutual Industry by AMFI a sharp increase is not only observed in total assets held by the Individual Investors, but the industry has also witnessed an extraordinary growth in the ticket size of their investment. The average ticket size of a retail investor has quadrupled just in time span of 10 years. The equity mutual funds have also been very well accepted and desired by the individual investors as compared to the institutional investors, because of its potential of wealth creation for its investors.

Graph showing share of AUM from B15 and T15 cities from March 2015 to March 2019.

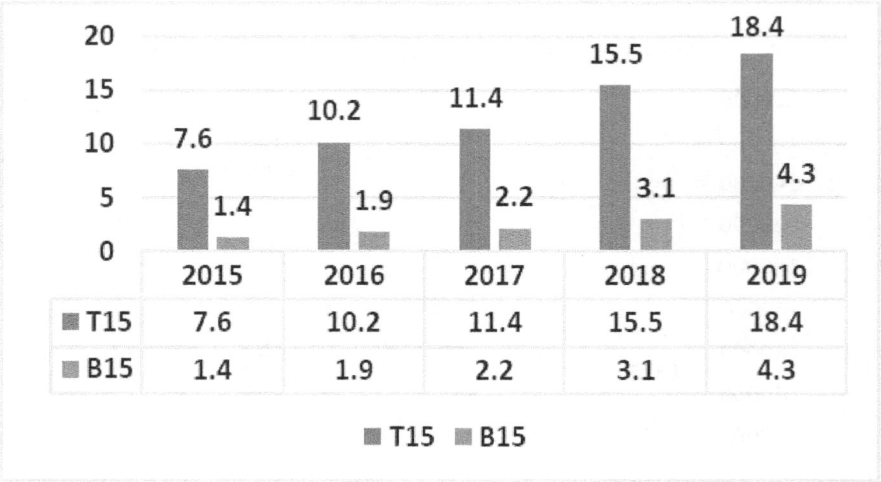

	2015	2016	2017	2018	2019
T15	7.6	10.2	11.4	15.5	18.4
B15	1.4	1.9	2.2	3.1	4.3

Source: AMFI **(AUM in Trillion Rs)**

The growth of the mutual fund industry is now not only restricted to T15 cities, but the industry has also in semi-rural and rural areas as well. The AMC's distribution channels have played a crucial role in tapping the investors from B.15 cities. IFA's are also contributing a lot to penetrate the market. AMFI is also working and focused on investors education programs.

Average Holding period for Equity scheme's V/s Non-Equity Schemes as on June 30th, 2020.

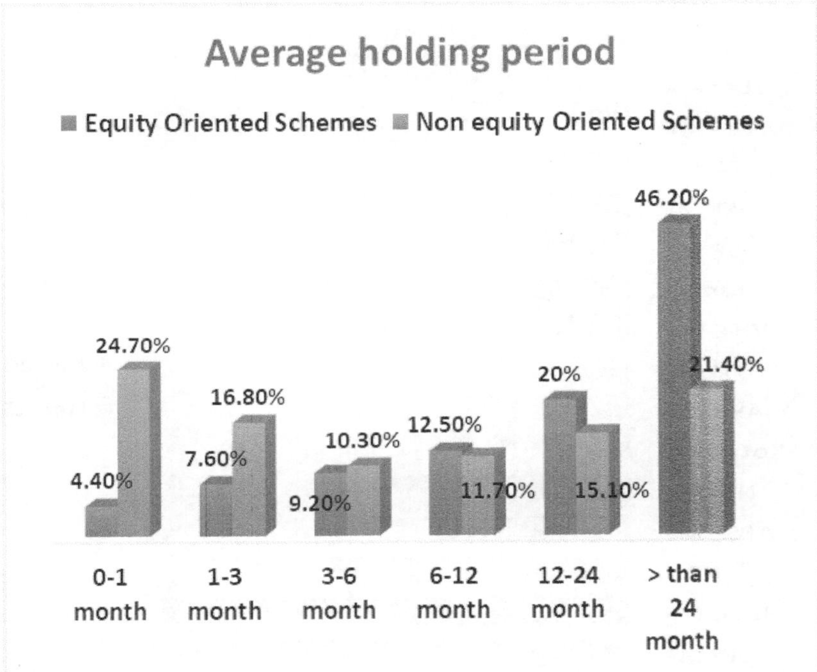

Source: AMFI

The above chart unveils the average holding period by the investors for Equity oriented and non-equity mutual fund schemes. It is evident that the Average holding period for equity-oriented schemes is 46.20%, which is double than that for the non-equity assets, that is just 21.40%. This refers that the equity assets are held by the investors for more than 2 years, and rational behind it is the potential and ability of Equity Oriented Schemes for creating wealth for its investors, if invested for a longer period of time.

Contribution of Top 15 AMC's to the total AUM of the Mutual Fund Industry.

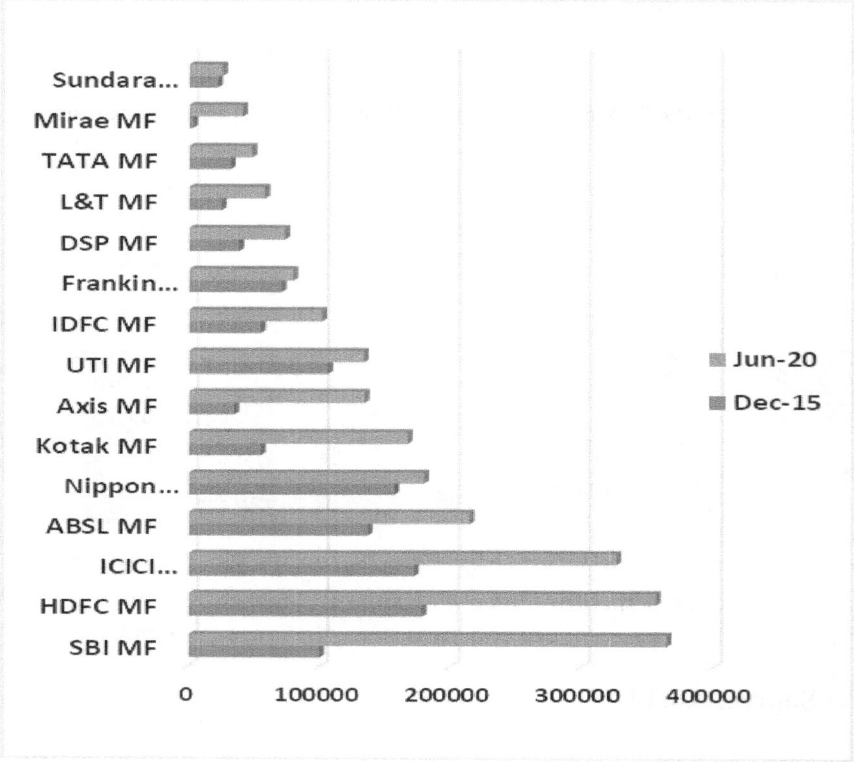

Source: Money control **(Rs. in CR)**

The above chart depicts the contribution by the top 15 AMC's to the total Assets of the Mutual Fund industry from December 2015 to June 2020. The top contributor AMC is, SBI Mutual Fund, followed by HDFC Mutual fund, ICICI Prudential Mutual Fund, ABSL Mutual Fund and Nippon India Mutual Fund, which are the top 5 contributors to the Industry's AUM. However, the most surprising thing is to notice the increased contribution from December 2015 to June 2020.

The percentage increase in the contribution to AUM for SBI Mutual Fund is 264.16%, Kotak Mutual Fund is 204.77%, Axis Mutual Fund is 289.44%, L& T Mutual Fund is 132.9%, whereas a whopping increase is observed in Mirae Asset Mutual Fund i.e. 1362.97%. SBI Mutual Fund is the largest contributor to the total assets of the entire mutual fund industry during these five years period. The least growth is observed in case of Sundaram Mutual Funds.

Chapter 5

Future Trends in Mutual Fund Industry

Indian Mutual Fund industry is undeniably one of the fastest growing economy as compared with other developing economics and other global economies as well. Even though the industry has observed stupendous growth in the last 20 years, still there are certain challenges the industry has to overcome in the coming years.

With growing formalization and financialization of the Indian economy, household savings have been shifting from physical assets to financial assets and within financial assets, from bank deposits to securities. As investment in capital market instruments involves risks, and individual investors lack expertise with regard to portfolio construction, stock selection and market timing, MFs step in to pool money from a wide cross-section of investors and diversify risk by investing in a portfolio of stocks, bonds and/or money market instruments. These investments are actively managed by professional portfolio managers who undertake strategic transactions to take advantage of current or expected market conditions.

In the process, MFs provide a steady flow of income and capital appreciation along with tax benefits to otherwise risk averse lay investors. Not surprisingly, therefore, household preference for MFs over other avenues of investment has increased dramatically since 2016. While the penetration of the MF industry in India, as measured by the AUM/GDP ratio, is still low compared with the global average, favorable demographics, a history of high savings propensity and regulatory reforms brighten the outlook for the industry.

In addition, MFs play an important role in equity, debt and money markets as efficient allocators of resources. The debt portfolio of MFs mainly comprises corporate debt instruments, which include floating rate bonds (FRBs), non-convertible

debentures (NCDs) and PSU bonds. In the money market segment, MFs are the major lenders in the collateralized borrowing and lending obligation (CBLO) segment, accounting for over 60 per cent of lending in this segment. As major domestic institutional investors, they operate in both primary and secondary segments of the capital market, providing a buffer against market volatility.

The lower interest rates offered by banks and post offices, gold and real estate becoming grim and unappealing, the Indian investors are becoming more inclined towards investing in mutual funds, because of its variety of benefits. Mutual Funds are not only capable of generating regular income, but also Capital Gains and Tax savings. The Indian Mutual Fund Industry is expected to witness a phenomenal growth in the coming 10 years. The growth and progress of Indian Mutual Fund Industry will be driven and based on certain key drivers which are as follows:

➢ **Attractive and Innovative Product Design**:

As mutual funds are becoming influential, and appealing source of investment avenue, there is a greater need of a variety of schemes, with diversified portfolios. These schemes should be capable enough not only to attract the customers but fulfilling their financial goals.

➢ **SIP: The Game Changer:**

SIP is going to be the game changer in the growth and progress of Mutual Fund Industry. SIP has brought a more controlled and pliable way of investing in stocks, without taking higher risk, and is best suited for the working and salaried professionals of accumulating wealth.

Considering the current data, the share of SIP in the total AUM is at all time high with 12.5% in September 2020. But, 7.6 lakhs SIP's have been cancelled in the past 4 months due to the COVID effect. The total contribution by SIP to the total assets of the industry was 3122 crores in 2016-2017, which had drastically increased by 8376 crores in the year 2019-2020. SIP is one of the most powerful tool in the hands of the industry to tap the rural markets (B 15 cities), as the minimum amount of investment is as low as 100 rupees in some of the SIP offered by AMC's.

➢ **Adoption of appropriate technology:**

Technology will play a pivotal and decisive role to bring about a revolution in the Mutual Fund industry in the years to come. Artificial Intelligence, Big Data, Data Mining and Cloud Computing will be essential and prominent the way in which mutual fund industry operates. It will lead to make the investment process effortless and uncomplicated. Regulatory bodies such as SEBI and AMFI are in favor of transforming the industry digitally.

The Indian Mutual Fund Industry despite of its tremendous growth still have to overcome many roadblocks and hurdles to reach at the level of growth at par to USA and Europe. There is no doubt that the 10-year CAGR of Indian Mutual fund industry is comparatively higher than USA, Europe and other ASIA Pacific countries.

Still there are many factors which needs to be taken care of such as:

- Improving the distribution model and its quality.
- To be in tune with global standards, markets, products and governance.
- Practicing continuation for investors awareness.
- Training and Preparing an efficient cadre of distributors.
- To bring higher managerial and operational efficiency, to cut down the costs.
- Use of appropriate technology.

When we evaluate and anatomize the mutual fund industry from the perspective of GDP or household savings, the contribution of the industry has remained small but importantly has grown as rapidly in the past two decades. All other alternatives such as real estate, gold, deposits have consistently outstripped the industry flows. The industry has not achieved its rightful position in the basket of options confronting an investor; therein lies a huge growth opportunity.

In variety any of the industry has shaped itself into a mutual fund industry rather than an asset management industry as defined by global peers. There exists an opportunity to offer products that address multiple investor needs. Taking a cue from global trends, not only does there lie an opportunity to tap into management of pension and insurance funds, but also to increase the penetration of products such as ETFs. Additionally, while asset managers in India are the largest Indian asset managers, they are not necessarily the largest managers of Indian assets - tax certainty and a push by the industry can open the doors for turning India an international asset management hub. There is an opportunity for the mutual fund industry to morph itself into a broader asset management industry. This will bring in additional investors and flows as the product basket will offer a holistic array of products with myriad combinations of risk-reward, attracting different classes of investors. An investor then will likely be offered a product that meets his or her needs at every point in life.

Chapter 6
Why Mutual Funds?

One can create wealth by deciding the right investment option to reach the financial goals. Mutual Fund is one such investment instrument will help the investors to invest their money in blue-chip companies in the stock market.

The money invested in mutual funds in invested in a large number of companies which will help to grow the money by minimizing the risk.

Investing directly in the stock market is not only risky but also a very huge, time consuming, and a tedious task. A fund manager takes care of your unit trust investments watching the market, selecting investments and adjusting the mix continuously. With access to investment information and research, he can decide on the fund's strategy and make sharp long-term decisions to manage the funds.

It is first important to understand what mutual funds are. Mutual funds are a pot of money contributed by different investors and are managed by an individual or group.

Funds and other investment instruments are divided into shares. Shares are a portion of the fund itself. This is what you are purchasing when you invest in a fund—a share (or portion of a fund) that will grow or shrink in value with the value of the entire fund.

Moreover, the duration ranges from one day to a lifetime as funds are invested across asset classes like gold, equities, long-term bonds, short-term bonds & cash. The schemes are also designed as per the investors risk taking capacity.

People have different dreams & goals and mutual funds can help realize them through a range of different products available. Be it your child's education, buying a house, retirement planning, and second income generation, creating an emergency corpus, planning a vacation, creating a corpus over a period or just saving money for the short term.

Building a portfolio of mutual funds is similar to building a house: There are different kinds of strategies, designs, tools, and building materials; but each structure shares some basic features.

To build the best portfolio of mutual funds, you must follow the advice, "**Don't put all your eggs in one basket:**" A structure that can stand the test of time requires a smart design, a strong foundation and a simple combination of mutual funds that work well for your needs.

One should begin with the a large-cap stock fund which represents the largest portion of your portfolio and builds around the large cap funds, which will each represent smaller portions of your portfolio. With a large-cap stock fund as your base, different types of funds will complete the structure of your mutual fund portfolio. These other funds can include mid-cap stock, small-cap stock, fixed income, balanced, ETF's and ELSS depending upon the financial needs of the investors.

Before choosing your funds, you need to have a good idea of, the risk appetite you can digest. Your risk tolerance is a measure of how much volatility in terms of risk and return one can handle.

Once you determine your level of risk tolerance, you can determine your asset allocation, which is the mix of investment assets—stocks, bonds, and cash—that comprises your portfolio. The proper asset allocation will reflect your level of risk tolerance, which can be described as either aggressive (high tolerance for risk), moderate (medium risk tolerance), or conservative (low-risk tolerance). The higher your risk tolerance, the more stocks you will have in relation to bonds and cash in your portfolio; and the lower your risk tolerance, the lower your percentage of stocks in relation to bonds and cash.

The importance of Financial Planning couldn't have been summed up better than this. Financial Planning is a tool through which one can chalk out definite plans in order to achieve one's financial goals, ensuring peace of mind at various stages of life cycle. In today's era of uncertainties, complexities and competition for survival, investment has become a crucial part of everyone's life. The recent economic turmoil has made a large impact no matter rich or poor, big or small. People have realized the importance of savings and right investment. A right investment is one which provides the right rate of return and reduces the risk involved in it.

WHAT IS THE DIFFERENCE BETWEEN SHARES AND MUTUAL FUNDS?

Shares refers to the units of the ownership interest which a person holds representing the equal proportion in the capital of the company and they are more riskier when compared with the mutual funds as they are vulnerable to changes in the market conditions whereas the mutual funds refers to the investment schemes in which the amount of money is collected by the fund houses which are invested in diversified areas and the same are less riskier because of the diversification as the money is invested in the diversified areas thereby compensating the performance of one security with other and reducing the overall risk.

When we invest in an individual share, the risk is higher. We expect the percentage to do well shortly, but if unfortunately, it doesn't, we lose a handsome amount of money. Now, what if, as an investor, we invest the same amount of money in the mutual funds instead of individual share? It will be beneficial for us if one share doesn't yield better returns, another will. The diversification will help us pare down the risk as much as we can. Plus, investing in mutual funds is much more convenient. You don't need to pick up the top 20 high-performing shares. The experts are hired by mutual fund companies to help you select. As a result, you pay a monthly amount, and at the end of a few years, you earn a great return on your investments.

A mutual fund isn't exactly a type of security, but rather a scheme that allows the purchase of securities. This scheme is professionally managed that pools money from multiple investors and places the money in multiple investments. The term mutual fund has no legal definition and is applied to collective investment vehicles that are regulated and sold to the general public. These companies are run by people with the know-how of the financial markets. They take the money and invest it in various shares across many companies, this reduces the risk of losing a whole lot of money.

If a person invests in a mutual fund, what the scheme will do is take 1,000 Rupees from 10 people, which would result in 10,000 Rupees and put split it equally in shares of 10 companies. In case, one of the company's share prices drops, it wouldn't result in one person losing all of their money but rather 10 people losing a small amount of their money. This is a far safer option, then purchasing shares individually. It also makes the share market open for the general public that may not have any idea about investments or how the share markets work.

Mutual Funds Vs. Shares:

- When you invest in mutual fund, your money is pooled and then invested in shares, bonds, etc. of several companies. That is, there is diversification but this is not possible if you invest in shares directly.
- Mutual funds are managed by professionals and all necessary research is done by them whereas if one invests in shares, it is the responsibility of the individual to do proper research about the company, price movement, etc.
- Mutual funds are sold as units and you are in no way connected with the growth story of the company whereas when you invest in shares, you become a shareholder of the company and may get dividends or profits if the company performs well.
- Risk gets mitigated in case of mutual funds as your money is invested in various companies but this does not happen in case if you directly invest in shares.

- Investing in mutual fund is easy. On the other hand, investing in equity needs more of your time and research.
- When you invest in mutual funds, you have no option of changing the stocks in your portfolio as it is completely maintained by the fund managers. While investing in shares, you can exit from a stock and buy some other stock anytime.
- To invest in mutual funds, you don't require a demat account whereas to invest in shares, you need a demat account.
- To get better and higher returns, one has to stay invested in mutual funds for a longer time period. While investing in shares, if you are a trader or a short-term investor, you can get better returns quickly if you use the right strategies of sell, buy or hold.
- Mutual funds have several other chargers like entry load, exit load, management fees, etc. When you invest or trade in shares, brokerage charges are applicable.
- Shares are a part of a business's growth strategy, while mutual funds are investment options for individuals.
- You can invest in mutual funds through a fixed monthly Systematic Investment Plan (SIP), as it is managed by a professional. You cannot make such a fixed investment in shares directly as the prices fluctuate constantly and need personal attention and prompt trade decision.
- Because mutual funds hold a diversified portfolio, negative returns are cushioned by the other stocks that do well. For example, if your portfolio contains 35 stocks, of which 3 are dropping, even the slightest growth in the other 32 will prevent your overall fund value from coming down. Direct investment in stocks does not offer you this protection and makes your stocks volatile. Unless you are dealing in a significant number of stocks at the same time, your money will be at high risk.
- Mutual funds have a longer-term growth strategy and will give good returns only after 5-7 years, while shares could give you quick returns if you buy and sell at the right time and choose high-growth stocks.

- In mutual funds, you need to pay fund management charges, a front-end load upon initial purchase, back-end load upon sale, early redemption charges, etc. In direct investment in shares you need to pay brokerage to the stock broker.
- It is easier to diversify your portfolio using mutual funds there are options such as hybrid funds. While dealing with shares, you may not be able to juggle with a large portfolio yourself.
- Direct investment in shares can give you tax benefits only under Section 80CCG, while tax benefits on mutual funds can be claimed under Section 80CCG as well as 80C if it is an Equity-Linked Savings Scheme (ELSS).

One has to clearly understand the differences between mutual funds vs stocks before investing in the stock market. With clear financial goals in place and with proper asset allocation, anyone can achieve their life goals.

What is Compounding in Mutual Funds?

Mutual Funds provide 2 types of earnings- Dividends and Capital Gains. If instead of withdrawing, you keep your earnings invested in a mutual fund scheme, you benefit from compounding. Compounding basically means that you earn returns not only on your principal investment but also on the returns generated by that investment.

As an investment avenue, mutual funds are designed in a way to magnify the benefits of compounding. This is possible through Systematic Investment Plans (SIPs).

Here's how it works: You can invest a fixed sum in mutual funds regularly through a Systematic Investment Plan (SIP). This can be monthly, quarterly or semi-annually. You can select the fund of your choice, use an SIP calculator to calculate the return on your investment and make a SIP payment on the allotted date. Investing regularly through SIPs could magnify your returns over time.

While you can invest in most fund types through a SIP, you may want to consider investing in equity funds for long-term goals like retirement planning. This is because equity funds have the potential to offer better returns in the long-term.

The best part about SIPs is that you can automate your payments by giving a standing instruction to your bank. You can transfer money from your registered bank account directly to the mutual fund on the specified date. As a result, you don't need to worry about missing payment schedules.

How to benefit out of power of compounding?

As an investor, you can inculcate the following financial habits in your financial decisions to benefit from your mutual fund investment via the power of compounding:

- **Start Investing Early**
  The earlier you start investing, the better it is as it allows you to have a longer investment horizon. Longer the investment horizon, greater the probability of earning higher returns as investment risk gets reduced over longer time periods. So, in order to make the most of the power of compounding from your mutual fund investments, start investing as early as you can. If you have not started yet, start investing now!
- **Be a Disciplined Investor**
  Being a disciplined investor means investing regularly and monitoring it periodically. Investors should avoid ad hoc and abrupt investment decisions and follow a proactive and well thought out investment strategy.
- **Be A Patient Investor**
  Patience and investing go hand in hand. In order to earn good returns, an investor must stay patient and not act in an impulsive manner, reacting to every sudden stock market movement. This becomes more important for long-term investments when abrupt stock market movements are more in number and triggering in nature.

What is Compounding?

Compound interest or compounding means you not only receive the interest on the basic principal amount that you have invested, but also on the interest that keeps getting added to it. It essentially means reinvesting the earnings you get from your initial invested amount instead of spending it elsewhere.

For example, if you invest Rs 100 with 8% interest every year, then your principal amount is Rs 100 and the earnings, at the end of the year, are Rs 8 (8% of Rs 100). However, instead of spending it, if you choose to reinvest it, then your principal amount for the next year becomes Rs 108 (Rs 100 + Rs 8) and the earnings you get are Rs 8.64 (8% of Rs 108), which are Rs 0.64 more compared to the first year.

Even though this looks like a small amount, it can make a huge difference to your investments, if you let the magic of compounding work over a long term.

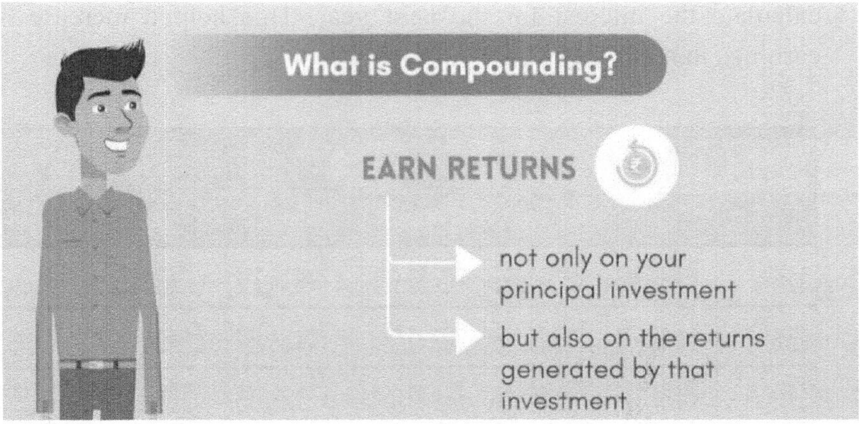

How does the power of compounding works?

Mathematically speaking, compounding is defined as, 'the increase in the value of an investment, due to the interest earned on the principal, as well as the accumulated interest.'

Simply put, it is a strategy that makes your money work for you. It could be regarded as a powerful tool to grow your wealth. You can use the power of compounding to plan your future goals, such as retirement.

Simple interest means you earn interest on your principal. But with compound interest, you earn interest on the principal amount as well as the accumulated interest amount over successive periods. Over time, this interest snowballs into a substantial amount.

Here's a hypothetical example to highlight the power of compounding.

Ram and Shyam both invest Rs 50,000 each in an investment avenue that offers an annual interest rate of 10% for 10 years. While Ram chooses simple interest, Shyam opts for compound interest (read re-invest).

At the end of 10 years, Ram would make a total corpus of Rs. 1 lakh. On the other hand, Shyam would earn a corpus of Rs. 1.30 lakh.

This is because in Ram's case, the interest was calculated only on the initial principal amount of Rs. 50,000. But in Shyam's case, the interest earned each year was included along with the principal to calculate the interest for the next year. This helped increase her earnings in a big way.

Returns	Investment Tenure					
	5 years	10 years	15 years	20 years	25 years	30 years
12%	₹4,08,348	₹11,50,193	₹24,97,901	₹49,46,277	₹93,94,233	₹1,74,74,821
15%	₹4,42,873	₹13,76,085	₹33,42,534	₹74,86,197	₹1,62,17,648	₹3,46,16,398
17%	₹4,67,906	₹15,56,130	₹40,87,050	₹99,73,295	₹2,36,63,131	₹5,55,02,041
20%	₹5,08,791	₹18,80,476	₹55,78,500	₹1,55,48,259	₹4,24,26,434	₹11,48,89,189

Fixed Deposits v/s Mutual Funds

Fixed Deposits are the traditional investment choice for most Indian households. As per RBI research released in June 2020, 53% of average household financial assets are invested in Bank FDs (as on March 2020). Though mutual funds have a long history in India with setting up of Unit Trust of India in 1963, popularity of mutual funds among retail investors have grown only in the last 20 – 25 years. As per AMFI data, AUM of mutual funds in India has grown at CAGR of nearly 17% over the last 20 years. Despite the rapid growth, RBI research suggests that mutual funds comprise only 7% of household savings. We will compare FD vs mutual fund so that investors can make informed decision on whether to invest in FD or mutual funds

What are Fixed Deposits?

As the name suggests, FDs offer fixed interest rate to investors for fixed tenures. FD tenures can range from 7 days to 10 years. Bank FD interest is compounded, i.e., you get interest on accrued interest. For example, let us assume a bank pays 6% interest (compounding annually) for 3-year FD. If you deposit Rs 100, after 1 year your account will have Rs 106. In year 2, you will get 6% interest on principal plus interest, i.e., 6% on Rs 106 or Rs 6.4. The additional 40 paisa are due to compounding.

A cause of concern especially for senior citizens who invest their savings primarily in FDs is the declining interest rates. FD interest rate has seen secular decline over the past 25 years (see the chart below). With RBI cutting interest rates aggressively in the wake of COVID-19 outbreak, banks have also reduced FD interest rates. On a post-tax basis, FD interest rates are now barely able to beat inflation. FD interest is taxed as per income tax slab of depositors. Since the FD interest rate is fixed over the FD tenure, there is no indexation benefits in taxation if FD vs mutual fund comparison is done. Therefore, there is no protection from inflation, especially when FD interest rates are so low.

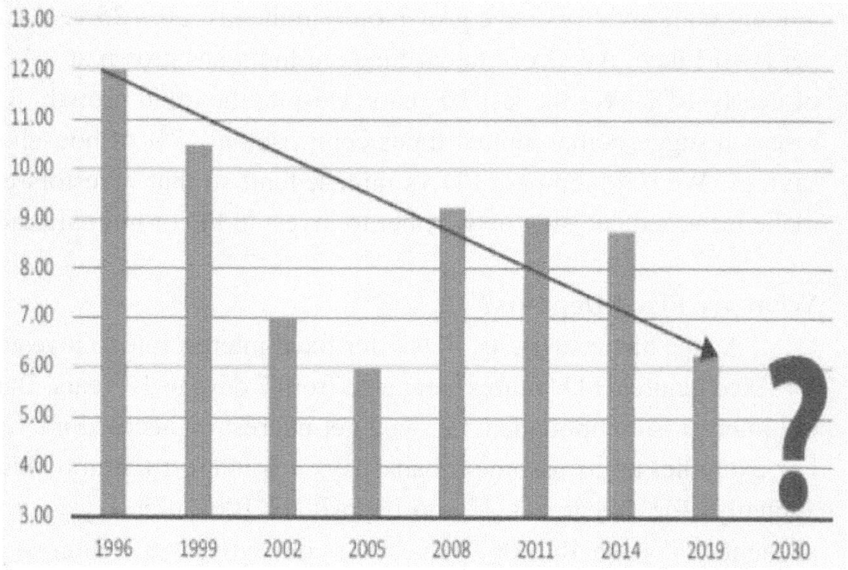

Mutual Funds vs. Fixed Deposits

Fixed deposits are the safest form of investment that guarantees a certain return. You can invest and never look back till its maturity date. Mutual funds too, provide different levels of safety to an investor –

a. Various levels of risk are available in mutual fund investment depending upon whether you choose equity or debt funds, or a combination. This information would be clearly conveyed to you by your fund manager. While equity funds tend to be more volatile and can give significantly higher returns, debt funds are more stable.

b. You can start investing in mutual funds with a minimum amount of Rs. 500 which will be managed by fund managers. In fixed deposits, you have to invest a minimum of Rs. 1,000 for 15 days.

c. If you withdraw money from a mutual fund, only the exit load is charged depending upon when you withdraw. In fixed deposits, you pay a penalty on interest on premature withdrawal.

No. of Years	Savings A/C	Bank FD	Equity MF	
	4%	8%	12%	15%
2	2,50,072	2,60,289	2,70,650	2,78,515
5	6,63,957	7,34,140	8,11,036	8,73,421
10	14,71,762	18,12,832	22,40,359	26,30,182
15	24,54,580	33,97,785	47,59,314	61,63,656
20	36,50,329	57,26,600	91,98,574	1,32,70,734
25	51,05,140	91,48,394	1,70,22,066	2,75,65,608
30	68,75,140	1,41,76,132	3,08,09,732	5,63,17,704

Mutual Funds vs. Gold Investments

Traditionally, investing in gold has been one of the most preferred options in India. Investors believe that gold can not only act as an investment, but also as a commodity that can be used when auspicious occasions such as marriages and festivals happen in the family. While this is true, we also encourage looking at mutual funds due to the following advantages-

a. There is a very high risk of loss in storing physical gold. However, there is no risk in having gold ETFs. ETFs are open-ended mutual fund schemes that invest in gold bullion of 99.5% purity.

b. While you can start investing in mutual funds with a minimum of Rs. 500, investment amount in gold depends on the rate of gold on the day on which you are trading.

c. There may not be any negotiating capacity while liquidating gold.

d. People often liquidate gold as a last resort when they don't have other investments to bank on. There are no withdrawal charges applied.

Mutual Funds vs. ULIPs

Mutual Funds and ULIPs contest for the same pie of market where they target retail investors and invest in market-linked plans. In the large-cap and mid-cap categories, there isn't much to choose between the two. There are lower expense ratios in debt mutual funds, which range from 0.28% to 1.48% whereas, ULIP debt fund options attract fund management charges of 0.65% to 1.5%.

Comparing mutual funds and ULIPs purely on the basis of monetary returns may not be appropriate. The fee of ULIPs includes mortality charges, management fee, and administrative charges. You may consider ULIPs only if the primary need is for insurance coverage.

Mutual Funds vs. LIC investments

LIC offers insurance policies whose primary purpose is to provide you and your family coverage in case of any illness or death. The purpose of mutual funds is to meet your financial planning objectives. If you buy insurance policies with savings or investment element in them, you may end up with very small insurance cover. This defeats the whole purpose of purchasing an insurance policy.

Mutual Funds vs. Equity

While mutual funds handle your money through an expert fund manager, equity involves investing in shares directly. Unless you are an expert in share market investing or intend to become one, it does not make sense to invest directly in equity shares. While mutual funds can give you decent returns over a longer period of time, equity shares give you very high or low returns over a short duration.

You need to constantly monitor the market influencing factors such as increase/ decrease in turnover of the company you have invested in, change in company management, the launch of new products, change in governments, natural disasters, foreign policy changes, elections, etc. Mutual funds are better covered because the investment is diversified over a range of stocks.

Mutual Funds and Tax Savings:

Mutual fund schemes for tax benefits help not only in reducing one's tax liability but also in growing savings over the long term. Such mutual fund schemes are called ELSS – Equity Linked Savings

Schemes – and as the name suggests, your savings are invested in equity markets.

ELSS investors have the savings locked-in for 3 years. Even if the returns are low because the market has turned turtle after the lock-in has ended, the investors may continue without exiting. As and when the market rises and NAV of schemes increases, the exit may be planned.

Mutual funds are one of the most attractive investments. A mutual fund involves the pooling of money in a variety of underlying securities. Units are issued to the mutual fund investors by the mutual fund house. The issue is done in proportion to their investment. Every mutual fund has an investment objective that is set out in the offer document. Profits or losses that arise from mutual funds are proportionately distributed to the unitholders.

Only SEBI registered mutual fund houses are eligible to receive funds from the public. There are various types of mutual funds in India. Some of the mutual funds also offer tax benefits. These are popularly known as tax saving mutual funds. Equity Linked Savings Scheme is an example of tax saving mutual funds. ELSS invests the investment money in equity assets only. It is also the only equity investment that offers such an attractive tax benefit. Investments in ELSS can help you to claim a deduction of INR 1.5 lakh under Section 80C of Income Tax Act, 1961.

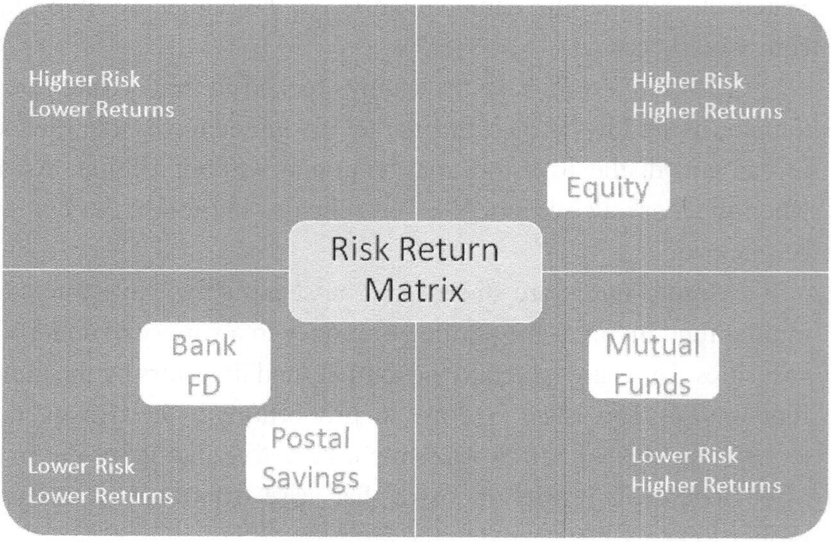

"If you are investing in ELSS Funds, you should not be worried about the past or current state of the market and think about the future instead. Not only are you getting an upfront benefit in the form of tax savings, but you are also likely to earn healthy returns if you stay invested for the long term as well,".

Benefits of investing in ELSS:

- There are no restrictions on the amount that can be invested in ELSS. However, the investments in tax saving mutual funds worth INR 1 lakh are eligible to enjoy the benefits under Section 80C.
- There is a three-year lock in period in case of ELSS. During this time, withdrawal or redemption is not permitted.
- Tax saving mutual funds such as ELSS are open-ended funds. An open-ended fund denotes mutual fund schemes that are continuously available for subscription and repurchase. These funds do not have a set duration of maturity. Investors can buy or sell the units regularly on the basis of NAV. These funds are top-rated among investors who are looking for liquidity alone.

- The total amount of tax benefits offered by tax saving mutual funds is capped at INR 1.5 lakh.
- Tax saving mutual funds are actively managed by a fund manager. These managers are professionals who ensure that the investment goals of the investor are achieved. Before an investment in any tax saving mutual funds, a thorough assessment and analysis is undertaken by the fund house.
- The portfolio of tax saving mutual funds is relatively diverse to minimize the risk from losses.

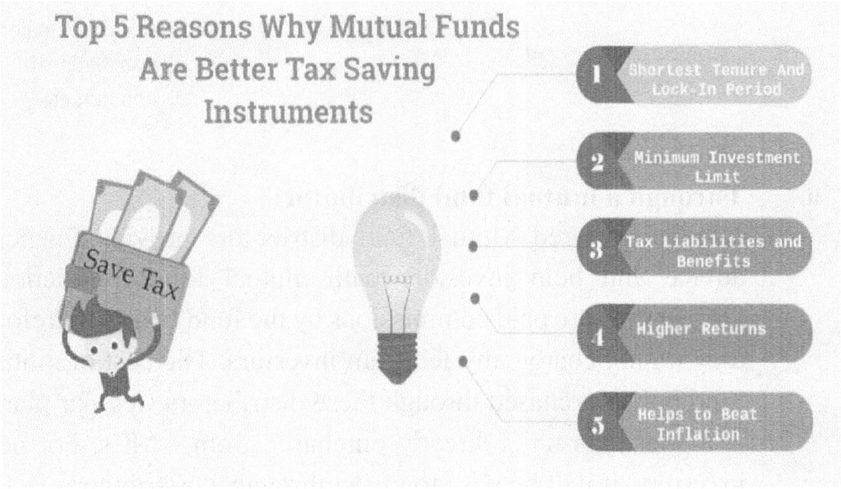

How to Invest in Mutual Funds:

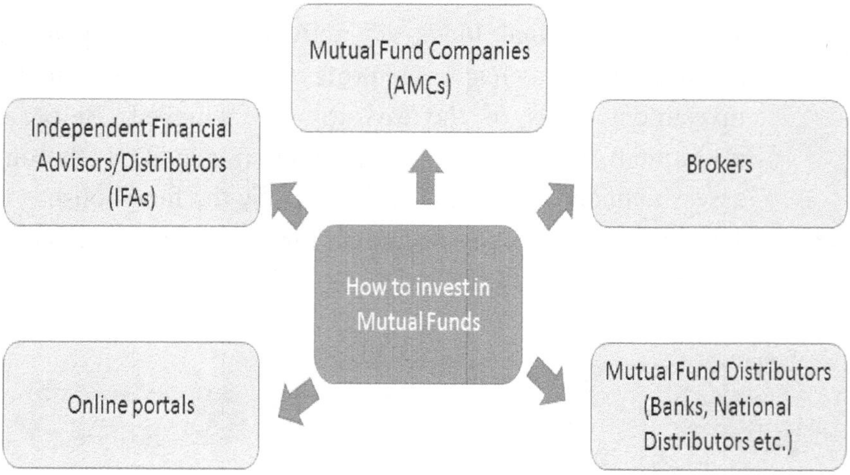

a. **Through a mutual fund distributor:**
AMFI registered Mutual fund distributors provide financial advice and help investors with mutual fund transactions. Distributors are paid commissions by the fund house; therefore, they do not charge any fee from investors. The cost of mutual fund units purchased through these distributors (regular plans) is higher than units directly purchased from AMCs. For new investors, it will be wise to invest through a distributor.

b. **Directly with the AMC:**
You can invest directly with the AMC by visiting their office or through their online portal. If you are a new investor then you need to submit your KYC documents either at the AMC office or online. You can buy direct plans, expense ratio of which is less than regular plans from the AMC.

c. **Through Registered Investment Advisors (RIA):**
You can invest through SEBI registered RIA. You can invest in direct plans through RIA and the RIA may charge you a fee.

d. **Through Registrars and Transfer Agents (RTAs):**
RTAs process mutual fund transactions on behalf of the fund houses. If you are transacting through RTAs, then you should

know which RTA services the AMC whose scheme you intend to buy. You can invest both in direct and regular plans through the RTAs.

e. **Online:**

Those who are thinking how to invest in mutual funds online have several options. To invest through online portals your KYC has to be registered. Some of the portals even help you in getting your KYC registered. All mutual fund houses also provide online investing option.

However, while investing online you should carefully check whether you are investing in regular or direct plans. You can also check with your mutual fund distributor if he or she is providing online investing facility through their own website.

f. **Through an App**

Asset Management Companies allow investors to invest in mutual funds through mobile applications in a quick and hassle-free way. The app enables the investor to invest in mutual fund schemes, view account statements, buy or sell units and check other relevant details pertaining to your portfolio. Investors can get to invest in a plethora of funds offered by different fund houses.

Chapter 7

Significant Terminology to Understand the Mutual Fund's Performance

Past performance of a mutual fund may not be a guarantee of future results but if you know how to analyse fund performance if you know what to look for and what to avoid, you can make better investment decisions, which can increase the odds that future performance will meet or exceed your expectations.

Apples to Apples: Compare Funds to Appropriate Benchmarks:

The first piece of information to analyse with mutual fund performance is the fund's returns compared to an appropriate benchmark. For example, if you want to see how well you fund is performing, it's best to compare it to the average return for funds in the same category.

Know When Good Fund Performance Can Be Bad:

If you are investing in a mutual fund, especially a stock fund, it is likely you plan to hold it for at least three years or more. Making this assumption, there is rarely a need to look at time periods of less than three years. However, this is not to say that short-term returns, of say 1 year, are irrelevant. In fact, a 1-year return for a mutual fund that is incredibly higher compared to other funds in its category can be a warning signal.

Yes, strong performance can be a negative indicator. There a few reasons for this: One reason is that an isolated year of unusually high returns is abnormal. Investing is a marathon, not a race; it should be boring, not exciting. Strong performance is not sustainable. Another reason to stay shy from high short-term performance is that this attracts more assets to the fund.

A smaller amount of money is easier to manage than larger amounts. Think of a small boat that can easily navigate the shifting market waters. More investors mean more money, which makes for a larger boat to navigate. The fund that had a great year is not the same fund it once was and should not be expected to perform the same in the future.

Understand and Consider Market and Economic Cycles

Talk to 10 investment advisors and you'll likely get 10 different answers about what time periods are most important to analyse to determine which fund is best from a performance perspective. Most will warn that short-term performance (1 year or less) won't tell you much about how the fund will perform in the future. In fact, even the best mutual fund managers are expected to have at least one bad year out of three.

Actively-managed funds require managers to take calculated risks to outperform their benchmarks. Therefore, one year of poor performance may just indicate that the manager's stock or bond selections have not had time to achieve expected results.

Focus on the 5 and 10-year Periods for Mutual Fund Performance:

Just as some fund managers are bound to have a bad year from time to time, fund managers are also bound to do better in certain economic environments, and hence extended time frames of up to three years, better than others.

For example, perhaps a fund manager has a solid conservative investment philosophy that leads to higher relative performance during poor economic conditions but lower relative performance in good economic conditions. The fund performance could look strong or weak now but what may occur over the next 2 or 3 years?

Considering the fact that fund management styles come in and out of favour and the fact that market conditions are constantly changing, it is wise to judge a fund manager's skills, and hence a particular mutual fund's performance, by looking at time periods that span across differing economic environments.

Check the Fee Structure of The Mutual Fund:

Managing a mutual fund involves costs in the form of management fee which is further broken down into other fee components. The fee also varies according to the plan you invest in; direct and regular. Regular mutual funds have a higher expense ratio as the investment is routed through a distributor as compared to direct funds.

A part of your returns is then taken as commission in a regular plan which is not the case with direct plans. Compounded over a period of time your returns are substantially reduced in a regular plan as compared to a direct plan. So, keep in mind these factors as well while comparing the performance of the fund.

In last couple of years, mutual funds have emerged as a viable alternative for Indian middle class. Mutual funds offer the best of both worlds. Since most of the retail investors do not have time and expertise to understand the stocks and businesses behind them, they find a responsible advisor in fund manager that manages the mutual funds. Second, the investors take advantage of booming equity market without investing in equities directly. Mutual funds diversify the investment into various equities and bonds and thus reduce the risk entailed in the case of individual stocks.

Ratios for mutual funds

Just like stocks, mutual funds have their own ratios that the investors need to look at to judge the investment worthiness of the fund. These ratios will help retail investors understand some of the key factors that impact their returns from mutual funds.

SHARPE RATIO

Sharpe Ratio is one of most popular and commonly used risk adjusted performance measurement technique. Sharpe ratio measures, that if the fund can generate excess returns for holding a risky security. The funds with higher Sharpe Ratios are preferred by the investors. Sharpe Ratio reflects the yielding capability of fund for the additional risk undertaken.

Sharpe ratio is an investment measurement that is used to calculate the average return beyond the risk-free rate of volatility per unit. In other words, it's a calculation that measures the actual return of an investment adjusted for the riskiness of the investment.

This measurement is particularly important when comparing two or more investment opportunities because it levels out the volatility in the market and flattens out the returns as if the risk was eliminated. Take a high-risk investment for example. This investment is much more volatile, increasing and decreasing in value much more, than a low-risk investment.

Assume that the high-risk investment had a higher return than the lower investment for a given year. Was this because the high-risk management or investment outperformed the low-risk investment or is this higher return simply based on the higher risk and volatility of the high-risk investment? You would never be able to know without this ratio.

The Sharpe ratio has become the most widely used method for calculating the risk-adjusted return. Modern Portfolio Theory states that adding assets to a diversified portfolio that has low correlations can decrease portfolio risk without sacrificing return.

Adding diversification should increase the Sharpe ratio compared to similar portfolios with a lower level of diversification. For this to be true, investors must also accept the assumption that risk is equal to volatility, which is not unreasonable but may be too narrow to be applied to all investments.

The Sharpe ratio can be used to evaluate a portfolio's past performance (ex-post) where actual returns are used in the formula.

Alternatively, an investor could use expected portfolio performance and the expected risk-free rate to calculate an estimated Sharpe ratio.

$$\textbf{Sharpe Ratio} = \boldsymbol{Rp - Rf \div \sigma p}$$

Where: -
Rp = Return of Portfolio
Rf = Risk free rate
σp = Standard Deviation

Sharpe Ratio will not provide any meaningful results to the investors if it is used in isolation, it provides best results as a comparable measure. This means Sharpe Ratio is only used for comparable funds. Therefore, a Sharpe Ratio of equity scheme cannot be compared with Sharpe Ratio of debt Schemes.

TREYNOR RATIO

Treynor Ratio measures the excess returns earned against it risk free rate at a given level of market risk, it is also popularly known as reward to volatility ratio.

Treynor Ratio = $Rp - Rf \div \beta p$

Where: -
Rp = Return of Portfolio
Rf = Risk Free Rate
βp = Beta of the Portfolio

This ratio attempts to measure the risk adjusted returns of a fund in relation with systematic risk. It evaluates the return on a stock earned for the level of risk assumed. The Treynor Ratio reflects the efficiency of the fund manager in balancing the risk return.

Treynor Ratio uses beta to calculate the risk adjusted returns of a fund and not the total risk of the portfolio. Moreover, beta is the indicator of the volatility of the fund. Higher the Treynor better is the fund in generating risk adjusted returns.

What Does the Treynor Ratio Reveal?

In essence, the Treynor ratio is a risk-adjusted measurement of return based on systematic risk. It indicates how much return an investment, such as a portfolio of stocks, a mutual fund, or exchange-traded fund, earned for the amount of risk the investment assumed.

If a portfolio has a negative beta, however, the ratio result is not meaningful. A higher ratio result is more desirable and means that a given portfolio is likely a more suitable investment. Since the Treynor ratio is based on historical data, however, it's important to note this does not necessarily indicate future performance, and one ratio should not be the only factor relied upon for investing decisions.

How does the Treynor Ratio Work?

The Treynor ratio attempts to measure how successful an investment is in providing compensation to investors for taking on investment risk. The Treynor ratio is reliant upon a portfolio's beta—that is, the sensitivity of the portfolio's returns to movements in the market—to judge risk.

JENSEN'S ALPHA

Jensen's Alpha is used to evaluate the return of a fund as compared to its benchmark index return. Jensen's measure the performance of fund manager i.e., their ability to outperform the market. A positive or a higher

Alpha reflects the market timing and good stock picking ability of a Fund Manager. A positive Jensen's measure reflects that the fund has generated extraordinary risk adjusted returns. A high alpha makes the security or the fund more attractive to the investors.

It takes into consideration the non-diversifiable risk i.e., beta. When two funds have same beta the fund with higher alpha will be selected, as it will generate high returns at a same level of risk. This evaluation is important because Jensen's Alpha evaluates the fund's managers value addition in the portfolio. It is also based on an assumption that the portfolio is effectively diversified. A negative value of alpha indicates the fund have underperformed the benchmark.

Formula

$$\propto = \boldsymbol{Rp} - [\boldsymbol{Rp} + \boldsymbol{\beta}(\boldsymbol{Rm} - \boldsymbol{Rf})]$$

Rp = Return on Portfolio
Rp = Risk free Rate
β = Stocks Beta
Rm = Market Return

The value of the excess return may be positive, negative, or zero. The CAPM model itself provides risk-adjusted returns, i.e., it takes into account the risk of the security. So, if the security is fairly priced, its actual returns will be same as CAPM. The Alpha in this case will be 0. If, however, the security earns even more than the risk-adjusted returns, it will have a positive Alpha. Negative alpha indicates that the portfolio has not earned its required return. A higher Alpha is always desirable by portfolio managers.

To accurately analyse the performance of an investment manager, an investor must look not only at the overall return of a portfolio but also at the risk of that portfolio to see if the investment's return compensates for the risk it takes. For example, if two mutual funds both have a 12% return, a rational investor should prefer the less risky fund. Jensen's measure is one of the ways to determine if a portfolio is earning the proper return for its level of risk.

If the value is positive, then the portfolio is earning excess returns. In other words, a positive value for Jensen's alpha means a fund manager has "beat the market" with their stock-picking skills.

Sortino Ratio:

Fundamentally, the Sortino ratio is a statistical tool that proves useful in measuring the performance of an investment with respect to downward deviation. This ratio does not account for the volatility in investment. It helps to represent a realistic idea about the downside risks that accompany a stock or a fund. In other words, this ratio helps to measure risk-adjusted returns of a particular investment scheme.

Sortino ratio is a suitable statistical tool for retail investors as they are more concerned about downside risks that accompany investments. It focuses on the negative deviation of an investment portfolio and its returns and thus offers a better idea about such a portfolio's performance after potential risks have been adjusted.

The Sortino ratio differs from the Sharpe ratio in that it only considers the standard deviation of the downside risk, rather than that of the entire (upside + downside) risk.

Because the Sortino ratio focuses only on the negative deviation of a portfolio's returns from the mean, it is thought to give a better view of a portfolio's risk-adjusted performance since positive volatility is a benefit.

The Sortino ratio is a useful way for investors, analysts, and portfolio managers to evaluate an investment's return for a given level of bad risk.

What the Sortino Ratio Can Tell You?

The Sortino ratio is a useful way for investors, analysts, and portfolio managers to evaluate an investment's return for a given level of bad risk. Since this ratio uses only the downside deviation as its risk measure, it addresses the problem of using total risk, or standard deviation, which is important because upside volatility is beneficial to investors and isn't a factor most investors worry about.

Beta

Beta of the fund shows the measurement of risk of mutual fund with respect to the market. In simple language, it tells you how much the mutual fund's NAV will move for a certain move of the market (generally represented by Nifty or Sensex).

If a mutual fund has a beta of 1.2, it means it will move 1.2 times the market's move. So, if the market moves up by 10%, the mutual fund's value will move up by 12%. If the market goes down by 20%, the mutual fund's value will go down by 20*1.2 = 24%.

A beta of -1.2 means that the mutual fund and market move in opposite direction with mutual fund moving more. For example, if market moves up by 10%, the mutual fund's value will move down by 12%.

It is a measure of volatility or systematic risk of a security or a portfolio compared to the market as whole. A fund with a beta greater than 1 is considered more volatile than the market; less than 1 is less volatile. Funds with higher beta signifies greater volatility and are considered to carry a higher risk.

If Beta is more than 1: It means fund moves up / down with the market with greater proportionate. E.g., if market goes up by 10%, then fund with beta 1.2 will move up by 12% and vice versa.

However, whether a high beta is good or bad depends upon the state of the market. If the market sentiments are bullish, then a high beta stock is better and if the market sentiments are bearish then, low beta stock is better.

Expense Ratio

Expense ratio is the cost incurred in running the fund by the investment fund house. The expense ratio is calculated by dividing the operating expense by the value of the assets under management. It is given in %. The expense ratio is a very important parameter as the expenses are taken from the returns and hence it lowers the returns that the fund earns. Needless to say, the higher the expense ratio, the worse is it for the investors.

Load structure

The entry load is, thankfully, no more applicable for mutual funds. Hence when you buy the mutual fund, you get funds worth full value of your money. However, the exit load is still there. Hence when you exit the fund or sell the fund, you have to pay the exit load. Usually, it is 1%. Some mutual funds forego even 1% exit load if you sell the fund after a specified period.

Standard deviation

It is used to measure the variation of a set of data from the mean or average. In the case of Mutual Funds, the standard deviation indicates the digression of Mutual Fund returns in different phases of the market from the average or mean as calculated prior. Financial advisors and investors use this data to gauge a specific fund's volatility.

- It tells how much the return of a particular fund is deviating from the expected returns based on its historical performance. In other words, it can be said that it evaluates the volatility of the fund.
- The standard deviation of a fund measures this risk by measuring the degree to which the fund fluctuates in relation to its average return of a fund over a period of time.
- High standard deviation denotes high volatility. For example: a fund with standard deviation of 10% will have a tendency to deviate 10% from its average return.

P/E Ratio

Price-earnings ratio or PER represents how much a single unit of a fund can earn and what price is to be paid for that unit. It is the ratio between the current price of a single unit of a fund and the earnings per share of it.

P/E ratios are used by investors and analysts to determine the relative value of a company's shares in an apples-to-apples comparison. It can also be used to compare a company against its own historical record or to compare aggregate markets against one another or over time.

R-Square

It indicates the percentage of fund returns that conform to the movements in the existing benchmark index. In principle, this method is the closest to alpha and beta ratios. R-square ratio figures lie somewhere between 0 and 1. The value 0 suggests that there is no percentage of funds in a portfolio reacts to movement in its respective benchmark index; whereas the value 1 represents that change in the benchmark index mirrors the movements in fund returns.

Alpha and beta, along with these ratios draw a complete picture of a fund or portfolio's history and forecasts solid grounds to make future predictions. Investors significantly benefit from these data as it lets them decide which best complements their investment objectives. R-Squared (R^2) is one of the statistical tools to measure the risk of a mutual fund. R-squared compares the performance of a mutual fund scheme to a given benchmark index. There are tools like alpha, beta as well, which measure the risk of a mutual fund in other ways.

A higher R-squared value means that the fund has a higher correlation with the benchmark. It means that a more significant part of the mutual fund portfolio is affected by the benchmark. A lower r-squared value means the reverse. It does not mean that a lower R-squared value is bad for a mutual fund. There are different types of mutual funds available. There are some, like index funds, where the objective is to map the benchmark index accurately.

Here, R-Squared will be naturally high. R-Squared might be lower for other equity funds where the aim is to beat the benchmark, and the portfolio does not precisely imitate an index's portfolio. Therefore, an R-squared number of 100% would mean that the benchmark's movement entirely explains the performance of the portfolio.

Chapter 8

Mutual Funds for Financial Planning

Financial planning is a process of setting objectives, assessing assets and resources, estimating future financial needs, and making plans to achieve monetary goals. Many elements may be involved in this process, including investing, asset allocation, and risk management. Tax, retirement, and estate planning are typically included as well.

Financial planning plays a crucial role in helping individuals get the most out of their money. Careful planning can help individuals and couples set priorities and work steadily towards long-term goals. It may also provide protection against the unexpected, by helping individuals prepare for things such as unexpected illness or loss of income. Financial planning may mean different things to different people. For one person, it may mean planning investments to provide security during retirement. For another, it may mean planning savings and investments to provide money for a dependent's college education.

It may even involve making career-related decisions or choosing the right insurance products. Many individuals choose to use the services of financial planners to help them reach their goals. A financial planner is a professional who provides advice and guidance for a wide spectrum of financial planning issues. Financial planners may or may not be certified and offer varied levels of experience. Though a financial planner may make developing a financial plan easier, hiring one is not at all a necessity. There are many books, computer programs, and other resources available to help individuals with financial planning. Furthermore, there is a wealth of related information available on the Internet. The decision to hire a financial planner may depend on many things, including the financial worth of the individual, his or her goals for the future, and the amount of research the individual is willing to perform.

All too often, people delay planning for the future. They may feel such planning should take a back seat to staying financially afloat in the present. However, even those living from paycheck to paycheck can benefit from financial planning by creating a budget. A budget can be used to determine what is actually spent each month and find ways to trim or even eliminate unnecessary or out-of-control expenditures.

The right time to create a financial plan is right now. No matter what your income level or what your hopes for the future, you need a solid plan to achieve your goals. Drifting through life without carefully set goals and well-researched methods of achieving them is a recipe for disaster. To enable your money to offer you more of what you want out of life, start creating a financial plan today.

Objectives of Financial Planning

Financial Planning has got many objectives to look forward to:

a. **Determining capital requirements-** This will depend upon factors like cost of current and fixed assets, promotional expenses and long- range planning. Capital requirements have to be looked with both aspects: short- term and long-term requirements.
b. **Determining capital structure-** The capital structure is the composition of capital, i.e., the relative kind and proportion of capital required in the business. This includes decisions of debt- equity ratio- both short-term and long- term.
c. **Framing financial policies** with regards to cash control, lending, borrowings, etc.
d. A finance manager ensures that the scarce financial resources are maximally utilized in the best possible manner at least cost in order to get maximum returns on investment.

Requirements of Financial Planning

Ensuring availability of funds: Financial planning majorly excels in the area of generating funds as well as making them available whenever they are required. This also includes estimation of the funds required for different purposes, which are, long-term assets and working capital requirements.

Estimating the time and source of funds*:* Time is a game-changing factor in any business venture. Delivering the funds at the right time at the right place is very much crucial. It is as vital as the generation of the amount itself. While time is an important factor, the sources of these funds are necessary as well.

Generating capital structure*:* The capital structure is the composition of the capital of a company, that is, the kind and proportion of capital required in the business. This includes planning of debt-equity ratio both short-term and long-term.

Avoiding unnecessary funds: It is an important objective of the company to make sure that the firm does not raise unnecessary resources. Shortage of funds and the firm cannot meet its payment obligations. Whereas with a surplus of funds, the firm does not earn returns but adds to costs.

Financial planning is a step-by-step approach to meet one's life goals. A financial plan acts as a guide as you go through life's journey. Essentially, it helps you be in control of your income, expenses and investments such that you can manage your money and achieve your goals.

If you take a closer look at the above examples, you'll find that there is one factor that connects all of them: money. You need to have an adequate amount of money to fulfil your goals and desires. More importantly, you need to have money at the right point in time.

For example, if you want to build up a corpus of Rs. 10 lakhs for your daughter's college education through investments, you need to grow this amount by the time she turns 18. Not a year later. This is where financial planning becomes essential.

Importance of Financial Planning

Below we have discussed about the importance of financial planning and why do we need financial planning. It will give you clear thoughts idea, Read below.

1. ***Income*** – When you have a financial plan, you manage your income better. You are aware of how much you earn from salary, interest earned, dividends etc. This will help you to understand how much you are earning and if it is enough to earn to achieve your objectives. (if you have a choice or if you don't have a choice at all)
2. ***Expenses*** – We spend money on basic needs, wants and splurge on luxuries. If we plan our finances, we will keep an eye on our expenses. Even if we go overboard in one month, we will know how much to cut back in the following months to stay within budget. Spending changes with changes in lifestyle and stage of life. This will help us determine income requirements and we can make changes in our earning capability accordingly.
3. ***Savings*** – You record your income and expenses in the financial plan. Therefore, you know your savings. Financial planning gives you an idea of how much money you need to achieve your objectives. You make a budget and therefore can assess whether you are within budget or overspending. This will help you understand your savings rate and how much you need to save to reach your goals.
4. ***Investment*** – A financial plan will help to choose the right investments as per your income capacity, risk profile, and goals. The financial plan will have an investment portfolio and asset allocation details. This can help you to have a balanced portfolio at all times.
5. ***Taxation*** – Thinking about taxes in the last week of March is not a prudent idea. With a financial plan, you can assess your tax outgo at the beginning of the financial year. You can plan your finances such that you pay the least amount of tax in a legal manner.

6. ***Retirement*** – We all want a carefree, relaxed retirement. It is possible only if you plan your finances such that your lifestyle is taken care of. You should have cash reserves to take care of medical expenses and other emergencies. A proper financial plan will have the retirement goals listed and the income, expenses and investment details. This will help you determine steps to achieve your goals. Check – Best Retirement Plans in India
7. ***Estate Planning*** – Estate planning refers to the provisions made regarding your wealth and its distribution smoothly after your death. The amount of wealth is not important here but the details regarding how assets and liabilities are to be taken care of is important. The financial plan will have a broad outline of what is to be done so that those taking care of your finances know what steps are required to be taken to manage your estate.
8. ***Ups and downs of Financial Status*** – There are many changes in our life. You get married, you can lose your job, you win a lottery or a loved one becomes critically ill. You make some money decisions that affect your standard of living. Such changes can lead to positive or negative changes in your financial status. Importance of personal Financial planning anticipates financial requirements in different conditions and ensures smooth financial flow at all times.

What Are the 7 Steps of Financial Planning?

The seven steps of financial planning start with getting to know the client's current financial situation and goals and end with continually measuring performance toward those goals and updating them as necessary.

Step 1: Understanding the Client's Personal and Financial Circumstances

The CFP begins their financial planning process by asking their client many questions designed to help them get a clear picture of who the client is and what they want. Some of the questions are qualitative and lead to a better understanding of the client's health, family relationships, values, earnings potential, risk tolerance, goals, needs, priorities, and current financial plan. Some of the questions are quantitative and lead to a better understanding of the client's income, expenses, cash flow, savings, assets, liabilities, liquidity, taxes, employee and government benefits, insurance coverage, and estate plans.

The purpose of establishing the goal or relationship is to form the foundation or purpose of planning itself. Financial planners do this by asking open-ended questions, which are questions that cannot be answered by a simple yes or no. Here some examples of open-ended questions you can use in your own planning.

Step 2: Gather the Relevant Data

The relevant data you gather is required to make recommendations for the appropriate strategies and financial products to reach your goals. For example, what is your time horizon? Do you want to accomplish this goal in five years, 10 years, 20 years, or 30 years? What is your risk tolerance? Are you willing to accept a high relative market risk to achieve your investment goals, or will a conservative portfolio be a better option for you?

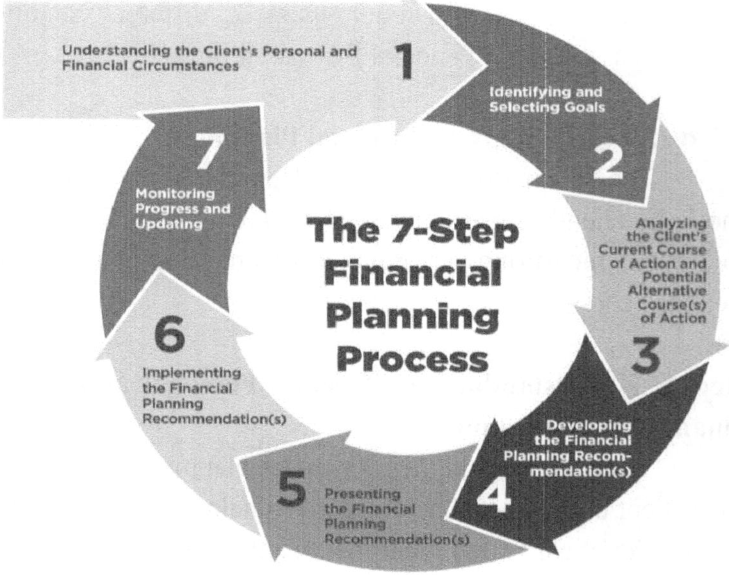

Step 3: Analyze your course of action and evaluate the status

A majority of your financial plan involves you analyzing your current status and adjusting as needed. Whether you are already on a good path financially or not, you'll be able to identify areas that can use a boost. Start with some simple basic questions about your finances and then expand as you get a good idea of what's going on financially.

- What's your current net worth?
- Are you cash flow positive?
- What's your net worth?
- What is your debt situation and what kind of debt is it?
- Do you have goals that you can reach or ones that you can't reach without changes?
- What is your plan to save money and invest today? If you have one?

Step 4: Developing the financial planning recommendation

The step 4 of the financial planning process, this is where you'll be putting action items in place to crush your goals and improve your financial health.

There are different areas of focus here, pending what you personally want to accomplish. But here are some places you can start. Set up where your money is going and how much. This can be for your savings, bills, and investments. Look at how you can increase your streams of income, improve your salary, and how you'll use that income. Is that through side hustles? Job hopping? Asking for raises? And how will you put that money to work? But also, understand what action items you'll take if you lose your job, income decreases, or an unexpected costly emergency creep up.

Start planning for other areas of finances that might not be so fun to deal with. Think about estate planning, especially if your assets get complicated and your family is growing. Plan for how you are going to be investing your money. If you don't have much cash to work with yet you can start investing in stocks. But your investing style should be based on your personal needs, risk tolerance, and goals. Keep it simple, look for low fees, and diversify. You'll eventually want to look into diversifying beyond stocks too, like real estate, bonds, collectibles, commodities, etc.

Step 5: Reviewing the financial planning recommendations

So, you have spent some time with your plan and putting action steps together. Since time may have passed and you might not recall everything, it's a good time to review everything.

Naturally, you don't want to get stuck in a cycle of constant tinkering but there might be things you want to adjust before implementing the plan. Talk with your spouse or significant other about the plan, get their insights or feedback, and ensure everyone is on the same page. If you are really unsure, you could consult with a financial planner to go over your plan or see if there are other recommendations you might be missing.

Step 6: Implementing the financial planning recommendations

After you have done all that previous work, your next step in the financial planning process is to implement everything you pieced together.

Typically, most people get gung-ho at the start, but progress can fade as it is easy to slow down or skip something. Then you tell yourself you'll come back to that step but in reality, that cycle continues. Flash forward to a few weeks or months that pass by and you're wondering where you went wrong!

Pending the actions, you will be taking, you will certainly need accountability. Create a budget calendar for yourself, set days for certain financial tasks or reminders, connect with a financial advisor or estate attorney, etc. The main goal with step 6 is to not set your expectations too high and start off your plan in attainable doses, which can keep you focused and motivated when you complete a task.

Step 7: Monitoring progress and update as need

While there are only 7 steps to the financial planning process, they do take some time to piece together. And even when you reach the last step, your work is not done! In fact, your plan may never officially be complete until you have hit every goal.

Additionally, over time your priorities and situations change, which will require you to pivot your plan or alter steps a bit. You might have created a financial plan with specific steps in the beginning, but your life can throw curveballs at you where your plan might not work as is anymore.

You'll discover areas in your plan that you had the wrong assumptions or thoughts. And you'll find parts of your plan may be incomplete, you had life-altering situations, or your plan has become a bit outdated. It's completely normal and is expected to happen during the lifetime of your plan.

As you can see above, there is plenty to do when it comes to the financial planning process. But it is entirely possible for you to succeed on your own! However, there are a few reasons why you might want to consider hiring a financial planner:

- You would feel more comfortable having someone you can rely on for expert advice when you need it.
- Researching and digesting financial information is intimidating to you and prefer to avoid making mistakes.
- You need someone to hold you accountable for your financial plan and your progress.
- You can get quick answers to all your money questions, without having to struggle through contradicting information online.
- Your free-time is limited due to work and family commitments that you won't have much time to build a plan on your own.

Currently, you own many appreciating assets and have a high net-worth where you need advice on how to best protect your finances.

Mutual Funds for Financial Planning

There is a hard-pressed need for financial awareness among people of different age groups, as the needs, requirements and aspirations of people tend to differ with age and so does the risk-bearing capacity of individuals. Life-stage planning generally encapsulates three important phases of your financial life: wealth accumulation, wealth creation. The first stage of wealth accumulation starts from the time you start earning and are able to invest money to build a secure financial future.

While this phase runs through your entire working life, it assumes more importance at the very beginning of your career. Once you have taken a step towards wealth accumulation, the wealth creation phase takes over, focusing on growing your wealth on the back of returns from the investments made over time. Wealth creation tends to happen over long term, as investments need their own time to consolidate and grow. Wealth creation focuses more on 'time in the market'.

Planning for the future and financial security are becoming crucial for all because of life's increasing complexities. For Indians, financial planning has been mostly synonymous with buying a plot of land, gold jewellery or putting surplus cash in bank deposits and post office schemes. But with time, people have started to realize that this may not be enough – life's various needs have to be assessed individually and each approached with a viable financial plan. We find that a busy lifestyle and being less conversant deter many from choosing the right investment product. Mutual funds can take care of this to a large extent.

Different mutual fund products offer unique risk-return propositions suited for investors with varying risk appetites. Investors also get to leverage the skills and expertise of professional fund managers at a nominal cost. To present a broad-based idea regarding how mutual funds can aid life-stage planning, we will divide an individual's lifespan into different stages based on age, and identify common financial goals. Then, depending on the life stage and risk appetite of the investor, we will try to identify relevant mutual fund products to meet his/her financial goals.

Stages of life and financial goals:

Young single – Age group of 20-25 years. At this stage the individual is still completing higher studies or has just got his/her first job. Around this time, common financial goals could be paying off education loans, starting to contribute towards family expenditures, building a corpus for marriage or purchase of house.

Young married – Around 25-30 years of age. This is the time when an individual is newly married and probably made the first big job change or received the first big promotion. S/he would be buying a house, a car, household gadgets, or taking the first foreign vacation.

Married with young children – This is between 30-40 years of age, when an individual becomes a parent. This is the time for frequent job changes and starting off on business ventures. Financial goals would be to support young children and aging parents, and buy a bigger house or car.

Middle aged – Between 40-50 years of age. This is the time when an individual's career is at its peak and it's also the time for inheritances. People would typically support children, plan for children's higher education or marriage, take vacations, and start retirement planning.

Pre-retirement – Mostly in the 50-60 age bracket. This is the time when the individual holds a high job position, has most debts paid off, and sees children slowly become financially independent. It's the time for wealth creation, children's marriage, higher medical bills, dream holidays, and fervent retirement planning.

Retired – Above 60 years of age. This is the time to retire from active work life. By now, children would be grown up and independent, health issues of self and spouse will become pronounced, and estate planning will be in progress. Financial goals would be to ensure there is no risk of running out of money in case of long-life spans, taking care of medical emergencies, and leading a life of leisure.

Cash Flow Planning:

Cash Flow refers to inflow and outflow of money. For better financial planning, one should keep a check on his income and expenses. Cash flow planning is a process where individuals calculate their present and future expenditures and strategize accordingly to achieve their financial goals.

Cash flow planning ensures that an individual has appropriate savings in case of emergencies. Therefore, this should be the first step in one's financial planning. An individual also gets to know how much disposable income remains for investment and other avenues after necessary expenditures are taken care of.

Investment Planning

Investment Planning is a process of identifying one's goals in life and correspondingly prioritizing them. In the long run, if you want to accumulate a good corpus of wealth, it is extremely important to invest in different financial instruments early in your life. These financial instruments could be equities, debt securities, mutual funds, fixed deposits, a small savings scheme, etc. Long term investment in some specific savings vehicles like mutual funds, yields good returns at maturity because of the compounding effect.

Tax Planning

Tax minimization and proper tax-planning should be everyone's priority if one wants to expand his/her wealth. You can invest in various tax-saving instruments to minimize your taxable income. This will help you in two ways, one, you would gain returns on your investment and two, you will benefit from tax deductions and tax exemptions.

There are many tax savings schemes started by the Government of India to facilitate investment in these schemes. This helps in the development of the economy as well as that of the financial markets. Many investors ignore tax consequences of their investments but in reality, taxes can eat up a considerable portion of your hard-earned wealth. Interest income from many traditional savings options like bank FDs and Government small savings schemes are taxed as per the income tax rate of investors. Mutual funds, on the other hand, are one of the tax friendly investment options in India. Long term capital gains (investment holding period of more than 1 year) from equity and equity-oriented hybrid funds (more than 65% gross exposure to equity) are tax free up to Rs 1 lakh per year. Long term capital gains from equity or equity-oriented funds exceeding Rs 1 lakh are taxed at 10%. Long term capital gains (investment holding period of more than 3 years) from debt funds or debt-oriented hybrid funds are taxed at 20% after allowing for indexation benefits.

Real Estate Planning

Real Estate Investment has long been considered as a low-risk investment with high returns. An individual could carefully analyze the market prices and the growth potential of the concerned place of investment, to invest in real estate properties.

Ten years down the line, an individual will surely benefit from the real estate investment. Also, in case of the untimely death of the guardian, a real estate property would act as a safety net for the heirs.

Children's Future Planning

Every parent wishes to raise their children responsibly with a bright and successful future. In today's world, doing that requires a hefty sum of money because of rising education costs and related expenses.

Parents should plan for their children's future beforehand and strive to achieve the set financial goal in time. This is imperative for securing their growing years and gives them a stable base of assets to begin their journey. We always dream to give the best education to our child but do we really think about the growing cost of child education? We want a child to become doctor, engineer or businessmen but do we really plan for it? As per me saving for child education is the most important goal for parents. Other goals like buying a car or buying a home can be compromised, but we should not compromise our child education.

As you know that the cost of Education in India is growing like anything. To meet expenses of higher education, you need to arrange more funds either from your own pocket or you need to borrow the money. The only way to finance your child education in the future is sound financial planning and investment strategy.

Parents need to plan for children's education

Over the last 20 – 25 years, with more and more graduates with engineering and / or MBA degrees entering the job market, the competition has been intensifying. Most Indian parents in the middle income or higher income groups have very high aspirations as far as their children's careers are concerned. Parents need to have a savings and investment plan in place over a sufficiently long period of time in order to meet their children's education goals.

Saving for children's education

One of the most important aspects of financial planning is to determine how much money they need to accumulate for their children's goals. You should always factor inflation in determining your goal. Once you know what your goal is, you can figure out how much you need to save to meet your goal. For example, if you want to create a corpus of Rs 70 lakhs for your child's graduate and post graduate education, 10 years from now, you need to save and invest around Rs 35,000 per month (assuming 10% annualized return on investment). The importance of an early start in financial planning can never be understated. If you have just 5 years to accumulate the same amount, you need to save more than Rs 90,000 per month.

Saving is not enough, invest in the right asset

The traditional savings options for long term goals were recurring deposits and traditional life insurance savings (endowment) policies. The average fixed / recurring deposit interest rate over the last 10 years is around 7.5%. Interest income is fully taxable as per the income tax rate of the investor. For investors in the highest tax bracket, the average post tax recurring deposit return was around 5.3%. In the case of traditional life insurance endowment plans of both Government and private insurers, the historical internal rate of return was 5 – 6%. In the accumulation phase of financial planning, the right asset class plays a very important role in ensuring success of your financial goal. Historical data shows that, equity is the best performing asset class over long investment horizons. In the last 10 years, Nifty 50 TRI, the benchmark index of 50 largest stocks by market capitalization, gave nearly 11% annualized returns.

Mutual Funds are ideal for education planning

Through mutual funds you can get exposure to equity and at the same time, diversify risk associated with investing in individual stocks. You can invest in mutual funds through systematic investment plan (SIP) where you can invest from your regular savings through automatic debit from your bank account on a specified date every month or any other interval. Mutual fund SIPs are the best financial planning instruments for your long-term goals.

If you investment Rs 30,000 every month through SIP, you can accumulate a corpus of Rs 65 – 70 lakhs over 10 years, assuming 11 – 12% ROI.

Mutual funds offer a suite of products suitable for different risk appetites and investment needs. For long investment tenures (7 to 10 years or longer), equity funds are ideal instruments for your financial goals. You can invest in large cap, multi-cap, midcap, small cap etc. schemes depending on your risk appetite. For moderate investment tenures, hybrid funds which invest both in equity and fixed income are more suitable for education planning. As you near your goal, you should switch to debt funds so that your goal is not impacted by market movements.

Retirement Planning

Every individual aspires to have a peaceful retirement without worrying about his/her finances. Financial independence is one of the key factors in why people plan their retirement in advance.

One should start saving for retirement as soon as s/he starts earning. It is crucial to have enough money post-retirement so that you can relax and enjoy the best phase of your life.

There is not a one size fits all approach when it comes to financial planning including retirement. Different people depending on their individual stage of life, risk appetites and financial situations need to have different approaches to retirement planning. Mutual funds offer a wide range of investment solutions for different investment needs and risk appetites. If you are starting your retirement planning at a young age, you can have maximum exposure to equity, including riskier equity sub-categories like midcap and small cap funds, which can potentially generate high returns in the long term.

Once you are in the mid-stages of your career with retirement and other stage of life, financial goals getting closer, a more balanced investment approach is more suitable and hybrid mutual fund schemes along with large cap equity funds are prudent investment choices. Once you get closer to retirement, you need to de-risk your investment portfolio up to a greater extent from the vagaries of the stock market and shift your asset allocation to debt mutual fund schemes, which may offer stability in returns and relative safety. At the same time, you cannot completely discard equity funds from your investment portfolio when you are nearing retirement or even after retirement because retired lives can be very long and you will aim to grow your wealth over time to fight inflation.

Wedding Planning and Mutual Funds:

In India, a wedding is the most important ceremony not only for the couple but for the family as well. Planning budget for the wedding is crucial as various essential cost like booking a venue, reception photographer, and sometimes even a wedding planner is involved in this. This all requires huge financial responsibilities, so you must have all the finances covered and plan how you should finance your wedding. You must plan your wedding sooner and have a good corpus in your hands to have the wedding of your dream.

Planning early for a wedding is always a good option than taking debts to have the wedding of your dream. You don't need to be aware of the exact wedding date you can always start saving from an early age. By an early age we mean you should have enough time to accumulate money for your wedding. You can save either in smaller amounts or in one or two lump-sum amounts. The aim is to accumulate an amount that will suffice your wedding expenses. The other reason for early savings is that when you have a lot of time you can also invest in financial products like equity instruments. Investing in equity instruments guarantees better returns in the longer run. Also, if you plan your budget now you can inflate the wedding cost and arrive at a figure which you will require in the future.

Importance of Mutual Funds for Wealth Accumulation:

Wealth creation for a secure future is the dream of every investor. However, not many do it successfully due to lack of expertise and sufficient knowledge. Although there are various approaches one can take towards wealth creation in the long run, the most practical and successful one is the mutual fund route. Most investors looking for high returns on their portfolio often look towards stock markets. However, investing in the stock market requires a high tolerance for risk along with a robust understanding of markets and stocks.

Equity mutual funds, on the other hand, make a great option for investors looking at wealth creation as they bring the professional knowledge and expertise of the fund manager, making them a much safer option as compared to direct equity investment.